THE SOCIALIST MOVEMENT

THE SOCIALIST MOVEMENT
1824–1924

ITS ORIGIN AND MEANING,
PROGRESS AND PROSPECTS

By ARTHUR SHADWELL
M.A., M.D., LL.D.

PART I
THE FIRST AND SECOND PHASES
1824—1914

LONDON
PHILIP ALLAN & CO.
QUALITY COURT, CHANCERY LANE

335

First published in 1925.

Made and Printed in Great Britain by
The Camelot Press Limited, Southampton

CONTENTS

Part I

PREFACE

THIS book is intended to be an introduction to the study of Socialism. It is mainly historical and explanatory, not controversial. The controversial literature of Socialism is enormous, the historical comparatively small; and what there is of the latter stops short of the momentous events of recent years. The best historical works, moreover, deal only with particular countries. There is no comprehensive and connected account of Socialism as an organised movement from its inception down to the present day.

Yet, like other movements, it cannot be clearly understood unless studied by the historical method, which traces the course of events and sets out in proper sequence the development of ideas. At the same time this method of treatment is not colourless. It subjects theory to the test of reality by placing them side by side, which entails a certain amount of criticism by reason of the discrepancy between them. When theory is at variance with facts the explanation involves criticism of the theory.

I assume that to-day, when Socialism has become more or less definitely the leading political question in most countries—and very definitely indeed in our own—every intelligent person must wish to understand it. I am sure that many do. One of the most eminent of living thinkers who has studied it—and come to an unfavourable conclusion—says "To condemn without understanding is useless" (Rudolf Eucken—*Socialism: An Analysis*). I would add that to approve without understanding is foolish. But a real understanding is not easily acquired; it demands serious study, as all the ablest minds that have attempted it have found. Socialism is not a thing that can be understood by the light of nature, though that is often the only light brought to bear upon it. Nor can it be mastered by running through a few partisan pamphlets or leaflets, even though they be on both sides. A background of fuller knowledge, and particularly a knowledge of facts, is needed to form a reasoned judgment.

I have here endeavoured to supply such a background within a reasonable space. That is my principal object. I have an opinion of my own and have expressed it, but that is not the main point. I want people to form their own opinions, whether they agree with mine or not. At least the book will, I hope, be useful for reference in regard to organisation, parties, programmes and persons.

If readers who know something of the literature of the subject find here things that are new to them, besides much that is familiar, it is because this book is not a compilation from others, but a study of original sources, matured by many years of observation and reflection.

I have to thank Mr. George Dobson, who lived for over forty years in Russia and witnessed all the revolutions, being imprisoned by the Bolsheviks for no offence and robbed of all his property, for kindly reading through the chapter on Bolshevism and giving me the benefit of his knowledge.

I have spared no pains to secure accuracy, but in a work containing so many details there are sure to be errors, particularly in the latter chapters dealing with recent events, on which information is difficult to obtain, conflicting and uncertain. I shall be grateful for corrections.

February 1925. A. SHADWELL.

INTRODUCTION

Some preliminary observations on the complexity of the subject are necessary to clear the way and explain the precise scope of this study.

Taken in its full length and breadth, Socialism is the most complicated, many-sided and confused question that ever plagued the minds of men. The confusion surrounding it is shown by the innumerable definitions that have been, and still are being, offered to the world, and by the endless differences that divide Socialists into groups, and still more groups, in an interminable series of sub-varieties. Seventy-five years ago one of the most distinguished French Socialists called it a hydra, because it had so many heads, and whenever it lost one two grew in the place thereof. He said that it was not a definite doctrine, but a collection of very different ideas and doctrines which were often opposed to each other and in a state of lively antagonism. That is not less true to-day. There has been some unification, but it has been followed by more division; some heads have fallen off, but others have grown.

The confusion is due to several causes, and much of it can be dissipated by recognising them and allowing for them.

In the first place, Socialism presents many different aspects. It may be approached from the historical, the philosophical, the ethical, the economic, the juristic, or the political side. Stress is sometimes laid on one, sometimes on another of these, and all are open to endless variations. It has even been treated as a religion, and it does, in fact, resemble a religion in its proneness to develop dogma, bigotry, intolerance and sectarian strife. It ranges in expression from a precise programme of action to a vague and impalpable 'atmosphere.' To some it is a policy, to others a theory, to others again it is only a broad aspiration and even a mere sentiment. This diversity makes it exceedingly elusive, and is of great advantage to Socialists in controversy, because it is always possible to shift the ground and to say, when any particular aspect is criticised, that it is not Socialism.

In the second place, even more diversity and uncertainty prevail with regard to aims and means. As to aims, some would go in one direction, but would travel different distances along it; some would go in a quite different direction; some would land eventually in a complete and rigid system of control; some in the abolition of all control. But the sharpest divisions of all concern means and methods, which vary from the most gentle and gradual process of change to the sudden and unlimited use of the utmost violence.

Besides all these differences between views bearing the same label, additional confusion is thrown upon the subject by the fact that Socialism has some features in common with certain other forms of thought and action which are yet quite distinct, but are often confounded with it. The most prominent of these are Christianity, State Action and Social Reform. Opponents of Socialism often call measures which they dislike 'rank Socialism,' though they have no objection to measures of the same type which happen to suit themselves. The relation of Socialism to Communism, Anarchism, Syndicalism and all analogous abstractions is another common source of confusion.

It is further increased by the practice of dragging in famous philosophers, moralists, religious teachers and imaginative dreamers of past ages, and writing them down Socialists, because they have said something in keeping with Socialism. When Plato and Jack Jones, St. Paul and Trotsky, Sir Thomas More and Tom Mann are tucked up together under the same blanket, labelled Socialism, it is impossible to say where such a very elastic coverlet begins and ends.

Finally, Socialism springs from and expresses the most contrary primitive motives—love and hate, greed and sacrifice, envy and pity, pugnacity and peaceability. It wears the badge of the gentle emotions, but makes most appeal to the destructive ones. In a book published in 1924 under the title *What is Socialism?* Mr. Dan Griffiths, the editor, has collected over 260 contemporary definitions of Socialism, which well illustrate the different ways of looking at the subject. The contributors, who are British with two or three exceptions, include nearly all the most prominent Socialists in the country. Socialism is described by different writers as a religion, a faith, a philosophy of life, a theory of evolution, a step in evolution, an historical necessity, an economic necessity, a new conception of society, an attitude towards life, practical Christianity, the Kingdom of God on earth, an opportunity for self-expression, an economic system, an ethical code, a class struggle, a spirit, a theory of political action, a theory of society, the opposite of Individualism, a tendency, democracy applied to industry, the science of minding our own business, a body of economic, political and social doctrine and philosophy, a scientific theory, man's mind developed, a criticism, a feeling, an ethical-religious mass movement, a system of political organisation, science wedded to art, common sense, a theory of national and municipal housekeeping, mankind functioning in the spiritual plane, a collective consciousness in humanity, the antithesis of Capitalism, the political and social faith of all sensible men—besides many other things. The list clearly shows how different aspects appeal to different minds and temperaments. The formulas supplied by the most eminent or prominent contributors must be given in full.

J. Ramsay MacDonald

'No better definition can be given in general terms than that it aims at the organisation of the material economic forces of society and their control by the human forces; no better criticism of Capitalism can be made than that it aims at the organisation of the human forces of society and their control by the economic and material forces.'

E. VANDERVELDE

'What matters at present is not so much to give a new and original definition of Socialism, but rather to find a definition upon which all Socialists can agree. From that point of view, and with that object, one can say that Socialism means the organisation of the workers for the conquest of political power for the purpose of transforming capitalist property into social property.'

PHILIP SNOWDEN

'Socialism is a system of industrial and social organisation, where the common needs of individuals will be supplied by the organised co-operative efforts of society, instead of the present competitive system, where such needs are, in the main, supplied by individuals competing to supply them from the motive of individual profit. The Socialist organisation involves the collective ownership of the productive and distributive capital employed in the socialised businesses. The method of management of socialised concerns will be by the ablest and best qualified men, under the democratic direction of the community.'

SIDNEY WEBB

'Socialism is not a system, but a conception of society. Its two fundamental ideas are (1) the substitution, as the motive for the fulfilment of function, of public service for profit-making; and (2) the allocation of the differential surpluses that we call rent and interest, not to private gain, but to the common good. The instruments for the gradual social transformations thus involved are (1) collective ownership; (2) collective regulation; (3) collective taxation; (4) collective provision—the whole under the direction of democracy, industrial and political.'

MAX BEER

'Socialism in its various phases consists of a body of doctrines and precepts indicating and urging a process of reconstructing society on the principle of national ownership of the material means of production and communal relationship between men. If democracy means the government of the political affairs of the people by the people and for the people, then Socialism may be defined as the control of the means of production of the people by the people and for the people.'

To these I will add one (American) non-Socialist definition: 'Socialism is an attempt to legislate unsuccessful men into success by legislating successful men out of it.'

It must, I think, be admitted that to see one's way clearly through all this confusion, to distinguish the essential from the accidental or secondary or irrelevant, to differentiate Socialism from other things having an affinity or resemblance to it, to put the ideas presented in their proper places in relation to each other and the whole—in short, to master the multitudinous intricacies of the subject and come to a reasoned conclusion, is a task of no little difficulty. Everyone who has attempted it with an open mind has found it so. A few catch-words and phrases, a few superficial arguments, which are the common equipment on both sides, are quite inadequate and soon exhausted; prejudice and passion merely blind the sight and distort the judgment. Yet these are the guides generally employed; they lead to bitter and barren controversy, but not to understanding.

A difficult subject cannot be mastered in that way. It may suffice for the Socialist, who is always attacking and whose most powerful weapon is an appeal to passion; but even he has eventually to justify his case by reasoned arguments before the court of public opinion, for which understanding is needed. Victory in sober argument goes to the man who has the most thorough mastery of the subject. The question is how best to acquire it in the circumstances explained above.

What is needed to find the way out of the confusion is a clue to the maze, which will take the inquirer past false openings and by-paths and lead to the centre, from which all the windings can be clearly seen. The best way to find such a clue is not to begin with arguments, but to follow the advice of Aristotle[1] and take Socialism at its origin, note the conditions in which it arose, the meaning given to it, and the objects in view. This should give us a clear and definite starting point, from which later developments can be traced, and some basic conceptions on which others can be built.

But what was the origin of Socialism? Are we to go back to prehistoric man (about whose social life our knowledge is pure assumption), Plato's *Republic*, the Essenes, the early Christians and all

[1] 'In any inquiry the best way to obtain a clear view is to start from the beginning and observe the course of events' (*Politics*, II.).

the rest? I think not. However interesting it may be to study these things and note points of resemblance between them and Socialism, they can all be put aside. What we are concerned with is the conscious and concerted movement, which had a definite and recognisable beginning a hundred years ago and has run a continuous, though chequered and disjointed course ever since, down to this day. This, and this alone, is Socialism in the proper sense of the word. It was, no doubt, led up to by previous phenomena—by particular utterances, speculations and proposals, for ideas precede movements — even by isolated and ephemeral experiments. Everything has a past, which can be traced backwards to infinity, and Socialism is no exception. But what we are studying is the living present, the thing before us; and it is a more than sufficiently complex problem in itself without putting in odds and ends from the remote past that have only an intellectual connection with it. To begin with, its birth as a living thing will be quite enough. But how are we to determine when Socialism in this sense was born? By the appearance of the term. When any movement, doctrine or cult becomes fairly established, it takes or is given a name, and conversely when a new name appears it signifies the arrival on the scene of a new idea. Their appearance is seldom quite simultaneous; the coming of the distinctive term usually occurs when the idea has had a little time to establish itself and to gather some disciples round its creator. But the one follows the other closely enough to give us an approximately exact date and the present study will begin with that.

Chapter I

ORIGIN AND MEANING OF SOCIALISM

Socialism, as an organised and continuous movement, was born simultaneously, but independently, in England and in France just 100 years ago. In fact, if I had to fix a precise date I should name the year 1824, which was marked by the occurrence of several striking events. It witnessed, in England, the foundation of the London Co-operative Society, which was the first definitely Socialist organisation; the foundation (in America) of the Owenite colony of New Harmony; the repeal of the Combination Acts, which legalised trade unions; and the publication of William Thompson's *Inquiry into the Principles of the Distribution of Wealth*, which laid the foundation of the economic theory of Socialism; in France the founding, shortly before the death of Saint-Simon, of the school of Socialism which bore his name and was the first French concerted effort to start the movement.

I think these events together establish the claim of 1824 to be considered the starting point; but of course, there can be no minute precision in such a matter, and it is open to anyone to prefer another date. Kirkup, in his *History of Socialism*, suggests 1817, in which some noticeable ideas were put forward; but these were isolated and not nearly so significant as the events mentioned above, or so closely connected with subsequent developments. However, it matters little; the period is more important than the particular year, and the main fact is that Socialism was born in the years following Waterloo. I will come presently to the appearance of the term and the meaning attached to it after reviewing the conditions in which the movement began.

They present a remarkable combination of circumstances. We can appreciate many of them to-day because we are experiencing the same. The nations had emerged from the war in an exhausted and impoverished state. The war itself, which had lasted for twenty-two years and been intensified from time to time by minor intercurrent wars, had thrown economic life into utter confusion, which was redoubled by the sudden change to peace. Heavy national debts, high taxation, disordered exchanges, depressed trade, high prices, low wages, unemployment and distress unrelieved save by charity and the poor law—these were the order of the day. In accounts of social conditions at this period, sufficient weight is never allowed to the effects of the war; but we can see from our present experience, which is very similar, how great they must have been. The acute and widespread distress that then prevailed, and the discontent aroused by it, were due more to that cause than to any other. Whenever trade took a good turn and the tension relaxed the troubles died down.

In particular, the economic dislocation caused by the war accentuated the evils connected with the great expansion of industry, through power machinery, which had then been in progress for a generation or two and is commonly called the 'industrial revolution'—a term first used, by the way, by Napoleon at St. Helena to indicate the supersession of agriculture by industry, not of hand processes by machinery. So long as trade was good the latter was welcomed, and indeed brought great prosperity, except to weavers. It created new industries, even more than it transformed old ones. It enabled young people to marry more freely, and so led to a rapid increase of population and a rising standard of living. Had it not been for the war, the material benefits would have exceeded the disadvantages, as eventually they did. It was the development of industry, and particularly of metallurgy and mechanical engineering, which gradually extricated us from the economic slough left by the war. Even the weavers got over their depression at last. I recently met an old gentleman, a retired Lancashire weaver, whose father had been a weaver before him and had lived through the transformation. He told me that at one time his father was paid 2*s.* 6*d.* for weaving 1 lb. of yarn, and at a later date only got 2½*d.* for the same output, but that he earned more at the lower than at the higher rate.

Nevertheless, the industrial development of the time, and the rise of modern Capitalism (as it is now called) associated therewith, entailed real evils peculiar to itself and independent of the economic troubles caused by the war, which indeed accentuated, but did not create them. It enormously increased wealth production, and opened up new ways of becoming rich to those who could take advantage of them, who were the owners of the new means of production. It created a large class of new rich, and the disparity between them and the wage-earners whom they employed was heightened by the fact that most of them belonged to the same class and had themselves been wage-earners. The assumption, made by Marx and written into Socialist literature at large, that the employers were already rich men who set out to take advantage of the poor is erroneous. Some were yeomen, who were not a rich class, but inquiry into the origin of any large concern started at that time leads, in the great majority of cases, to a workman at the far end—an exceptionally capable, industrious and ambitious workman, and generally also a hard man. Such men, who began in a small way and did not spare themselves, were the greatest oppressors of their fellows; they saw no harm in it, having always been wont to take all they could get. An anecdote related in the *Cotton Factory Times*, the trade union journal for that industry, reveals their mentality. A mill-owner of this class received a deputation, which asked for a rise of wages and reminded him that when he was a workman himself he always got as much as he could. "Yes, and you ought to know I haven't altered yet," was his reply; it effectually silenced the deputation, which sadly withdrew. In his place they would have done the same. If any evidence is needed, the testimony of the *Poor Man's Guardian*, the *Daily Herald* of that time, should be enough:

'How many individuals have been known to raise themselves to the greatest heights of affluence, rank and station in society; yet it is invariably the case that such men are greater tyrants and oppressors of that class from which they sprang than those who were born in affluence.'

That was written in 1831 and later experience confirmed the tendency. The annual report of the Amalgamated Society of Engineers for 1855 observes: 'We have found that when a few of our own members have commenced business hitherto they have abandoned the Society and conducted the workshops even worse than other employers.' (*The History of Trade Unionism*, by Sidney and Beatrice Webb, p. 207). And right down to the present day we have the same observation. So lately as August 1923 a correspondent of the *Daily Herald* wrote, in reference to the class war: 'I have learned that the hardest employers are those who have been wage-earners themselves.'

It was this class in particular that took advantage of the rapid development of machine industry, and grew rich and powerful. They were 'self-made men.' The ironmaster and manufacturer from the industrial North and the Midlands became a recognised type, and were always represented as very rough diamonds. Owning the mills and factories, they had great power over the workmen, which many abused.[1] There is no doubt about the oppression and hardship, particularly in the

[1] A note by Saint-Simon, in his *Letters from a Resident in Geneva to his Contemporaries*, is worth repeating in this connection. He begs the reader to ponder this observation: 'The owners command the non-owners, not because they possess the properties, but they possess the properties and they command because, taken collectively, they have more intelligence than the non-owners' (*Œuvres—Lettres d'un Habitant de Genève*, p. 27).

first quarter of the nineteenth century, when combination was illegal. The employers ruthlessly beat down wages when trade was bad, resisted demands for advances when it was good, discharged their men without compunction when it suited them, imposed excessively long hours on women and children as well as on men, resorted to fines and truck and other devices. The effect of these practices was greatly heightened by the abnormal troubles following the war and mentioned above. It was in these material circumstances that Socialism was born. It represented a reaction against the existing misery and oppression.

It was at the same time a revolt against the current theories of political economy, which were all in favour of the industrial development and against any interference with it. This was a third circumstance which combined to make the period exceptional. Political economy had recently become a very influential and authoritative branch of thought, and the importance attached to it marked the passing of Western civilisation into a new stage, in which material conditions took precedence of all others, and their improvement became the recognised ideal of the time. The Age of Reason gave place to the Age of Wealth, and political economy, as the science of wealth, acquired authority. The orthodox economic theory of the day was that of *laissez faire*, or letting things alone, the theory that free individual enterprise and free competition—otherwise free trade—would produce the best results through the play of natural forces and the survival of the best. It was itself a reaction against overstrained State control, and was put forward in the middle of the eighteenth century in France, where control had become intolerably oppressive and injurious, by the French school of economists called the Physiocrats.[1] But it was Adam Smith's famous work, *The Wealth of Nations*, published in 1776, that gave the theory the commanding influence it soon acquired. It was right up to a certain point, but its advocates were too sanguine and too partial, as advocates of new theories usually are. They expected too much from it and overlooked the drawbacks. They did not foresee that free enterprise and free competition, based on the principle of individualism, would have the results indicated above, which became so glaringly obvious in the years after Waterloo and led to the reaction signalised by the appearance of Socialism.

We have an admirable and impartial witness in Sismondi, who first formally challenged the economic doctrine of *laissez faire*, though he was not a Socialist.[2] He had been a disciple of Adam Smith, but observation and study in several European countries, and particularly in England, convinced him that

[1] The founders and leaders of the school were essentially reformers, high-minded and disinterested men, whose motive was relief of the poor and oppressed. The most famous of them were Quesnay, whose genius raised him from the position of an obscure medical practitioner to be the trusted adviser of the King, and Turgot, the eminent statesman. They did not invent the expression *laissez faire*, which had been used by Colbert (*Comptes Rendus de l'Institut*, xxxix. 93).

[2] J. C. L. de Sismondi (1773–1842), historian and economist; born at Geneva, of an illustrious Italian family, which had migrated to France in 1524 and thence to Switzerland in the following century. Brought up to business at Lyons, he turned his attention to economics, studied in England and Italy, as well as in France and Switzerland His writing attracted notice, and he was offered the Chair of Political Economy at Wilna, but declined it. Studied political science and history. Wrote a *History of the Italian Republic* and a *History of France*, both classics to this day, besides numerous other works.

there was something wrong with the theory of free and unrestricted competition, which had not worked out as its advocates predicted. He recognised the great achievements of industrialism, but also perceived its ill effects, which he described and examined in a work entitled *New Principles of Political Economy*, published in 1819. In this work, and in other shorter essays, he anticipated the leading ideas about the evolution of Capitalism elaborated by Marx nearly thirty years later in *Das Kapital*. One might quote pages, but a few references must suffice. He argued, from actual conditions, that the principles of unrestricted competition must tend to depress labour by forcing economy in production, which entailed either getting a larger output with the same labour, or the same output with less labour, or getting labour cheaper, which was effected by surplus hands being thrown on the market; and that every discovery and improvement—all progress in manufacture—tended thus to reduce the value and reward of labour.

> 'The fundamental change which has taken place in society, amidst this universal struggle created by competition, is the introduction of the "proletary" among human conditions, the name of whom, borrowed from the Romans, is ancient, but whose existence is quite new. . . . It may almost be said that in modern times the community lives at the expense of the proletary, on that share of the remuneration of his labour which it deducts from him. . . . The more wealth is accumulated in a single hand the cheaper can it execute the work it has undertaken. . . .

This principle, which creates an abyss between extreme opulence and extreme poverty, applies equally to all industrial labour, and it gradually drives everywhere out of the field that happy independence, that happy mediocrity, which was long the object of the wishes of the wise. . . . In England it is only by the immensity of capitals that manufacturers prosper. It is only where a manufacturer has much credit at his disposal that there is economy in the power of machines, in their durability, in the inspection of the work-people, in scientific works, in responsibility, in facilities of sale. Great workshops competing with small ones, have in every market an advantage in proportion to size.'

Here we have in outline the whole system of Marxian economics—wealth produced by labour, which is defrauded of its rightful share by capitalist employers; creation of propertyless proletarians; concentration of capital; small concerns crushed by large ones; abyss between rich and poor; the rich growing richer, the poor poorer. This is virtually identical with the preamble to the Erfurt Programme[1] of 1891, but written seventy-three years before, when Marx was in the cradle. Sismondi also propounded the theory of surplus value, which is the keystone of the Marxian analysis. Rent, interest and profits, he said, are nothing but 'the surplus of the value of what labour has produced above the advances that have been made to produce it.'

I dwell upon him partly because he is usually

[1] See page 57.

ignored, but mainly because he was writing at the very time with which we are dealing, and being a competent, judicious and disinterested observer, with no leaning to Socialism, though deeply sympathetic towards poverty and suffering (no one has pleaded more eloquently for the poor), he reveals better than anyone else the reaction against the doctrine of *laissez faire* and the reasons for it, out of which Socialism took its rise. The interval between the first edition of his *New Principles* (1819) and the second (1826) covered the date we have chosen, and in the preface to the second edition he says that during that time facts had fought in his favour and had proved that the theories he challenged,

> 'Wherever they were put in practice, served well enough to increase material wealth, but that they diminished the mass of enjoyment laid up for each individual; that if they tended to make the rich man more rich, they also made the poor man more poor, more dependent and more destitute. Crises utterly unexpected have succeeded one another in the commercial world; the progress of industry and opulence has not saved the operatives who created this opulence from unheard of sufferings. . . . I have seen production increasing, whilst enjoyments were diminishing. . . . I have shown that that equilibrium among the gains of rival occupations, on which modern economists have founded their calculations, has never been attained, except by the destruction of fixed capital and the mortality of workmen engaged in a losing

manufacture; that although the invention of machines, which increase the power of man, may be a benefit to humanity, yet the unjust distribution which we make of profits obtained by their means changes them into scourges to the poor.'

The case is clear. What he describes was going on when he wrote, and when Socialism made its appearance. It was, I repeat, a reaction—an extreme reaction—against the then economic order. Moreover, the classical economists themselves supplied arguments for the revolt in the theory that 'labour' produces all wealth and all value. This is the labour theory of value, on which the economic arguments for Socialism have always been based. It was first suggested in the seventeenth century, but was more precisely and authoritatively stated by Adam Smith and applied dogmatically by Ricardo, whose *Principles of Political Economy*, published in 1817, provided Socialists with an inexhaustible text. Chapter I is headed by the statement:

'The value of a commodity, or the quantity of any other commodity for which it will exchange, depends on the relative quantity of labour which is necessary for its production, and not on the greater or less compensation which is paid for that labour.'

A fallacy lies concealed in the ambiguity of the word 'labour.' Originally it meant in this connection all kinds of work or effort, and in that sense it is true that all wealth is produced by labour, if the share of nature be assumed. But this meaning was narrowed down, by loose usage and confused thinking, to the particular kind of work commonly called manual labour, and, read in that sense, the axiom implied a gross injustice to manual labour, which produced everything and received only a small share of the product. It was so read by Socialists, and not by them only; Sismondi was evidently deceived by it. The air of scientific exactness assumed by Ricardo lent it great authority and consequently it played a large part in stimulating the revolt against the existing order. To the actual suffering of the time it added a cry of injustice based on the teaching of the highest economic authority.

In addition to all this, other contemporary currents of thought swelled the stream in the same direction. One was the humanitarian movement and the celebrated principle of 'the greatest happiness of the greatest number' then in vogue; another was the ferment left by the French Revolution, which still pervaded men's minds and inclined them to seek a remedy for present distresses in large changes and a new order. This influence was naturally stronger in France than in England, and Socialism was commonly regarded by its advocates there as a completion of the work of the Revolution for emancipation, liberty and equality. In England, on the other hand, stress was chiefly laid on the purely economic side of the question, on account of industrial conditions.

To sum up, Socialism represented a revolt against actual material conditions, a reaction against the theory that went with them, and at the same time a demand for greater economic equality and more liberty for the employed in their relations with employers. It was primarily and essentially an economic movement; economic conditions formed the core and heart of it. If there had been no poor or rich there would have been no Socialism.

We can now go on to the name coined to designate this movement, and the meaning attached to it by those who coined it. Here it is necessary to distinguish between the terms 'Socialist' and 'Socialism,' which had a different origin; one was coined in England, the other in France. The facts having been repeatedly mis-stated in one book after another, it is desirable to be particular about them; and all the more because the inquiry gives us two illuminating conceptions. The earlier of the two was 'Socialist,' which was coined in England not long after the year 1824. The earliest use of it in print that has yet been discovered was in the *Co-operative Magazine* for November 1827. The discovery was made by Mr. Max Beer, when searching the files of early Socialist periodicals for his *History of British Socialism,* published in 1919. The *Co-operative Magazine* was the organ of the London Co-operative Society, which has been mentioned above as having been founded in the year 1824. It appears to have been an intellectual society something like the Fabians. Mr. Beer suggests that the word was coined in the debates the society was in the habit of holding, and no doubt he is right. The subjects of these debates which he quotes reveal the influence of the currents of thought indicated above; they include, among other things, the responsibility of individual competition in the production and distribution of wealth for the moral and physical ills that afflicted mankind; the right of the labourer to the whole produce of his labour, and the reasons for the poverty and wretchedness of the producing classes. With regard to the word 'Socialist' and its meaning I quote Mr. Beer:

> 'In a footnote to a communication of the Brighton co-operators the editor of the *Co-operative Magazine* observes that the value of a commodity consisted both of present and past labour (capital or stock), and the main question was "whether it is more beneficial that this capital should be individual or common." Those who argued that it should be in the hands of individual employers were the modern political economists of the type of James Mill and Malthus, while those who thought it should be common were "the Communists and Socialists."'

It is a remarkable fact that at the very outset of the movement we should get this clear statement of the aim of Socialism as the common or public ownership of capital; for this is precisely its aim to-day. It is the one thing on which the various sects agree, the ultimate residue distilled, so to speak, from all the theorising and discussion and argument of a hundred years. All demand the abolition of privately owned industrial and commercial capital and its transference to public ownership. They do not demand the abolition of capital or of private property, as many anti-Socialists commonly suppose, but the abolition of private property in capital, that is, in the means of production, distribution and exchange, to use the full formula.

This conception of Socialism is simple, precise, concrete and practical, whether feasible and desirable or not. And it is wholly economic. Time has proved it to be the central principle, the real core of the movement. All the other aspects are secondary, they represent arguments in its favour historical, ethical, juristic, political. If the central idea is clearly grasped, they fall into their places around it, and the whole subject is greatly simplified. If that conception had been firmly held all through, what a mass of verbiage, misunderstanding, vain controversy and contention might have been avoided! But it was soon overlaid with all sorts of fantastic additions and sank out of sight in a cloud of confusion. The next definition of a Socialist to be found in the literature of that time occurs in the *Poor Man's Guardian* in 1833, and describes him as one who 'preaches of community of goods, abolition of crime and punishment, of magistrates and marriage.' If the public acquired confused and erroneous notions about the movement, the fault lay with Socialists who mixed up extraneous and irrelevant matters with the real object.

The simple formula did not emerge clearly again from the welter of theory and argument until it was rediscovered with much labour by Professor Schäffle nearly fifty years later, in the second period of Socialism. He stated it in his *Quintessence of Socialism*, published in 1874 and translated into English in 1906. The first thing needed, he said, 'in view of the confused state of public opinion,' was a precise knowledge of the essence and aims of the Socialistic reconstruction of society. He pointed out that it was essentially an economic question and defined the real aim of Socialism to be :

> 'To replace the system of private capital by a system of collective capital, that is, by a method of production which would introduce a unified (social or collective) organisation of national labour, on the basis of collective or common ownership of the means of production by all the members of the society.'[1]

This is more verbose than the statement of 1827, but adds nothing material to it and even contains less, for the editor of the *Co-operative Magazine* got in the conception of capital as accumulated past labour, which is often and erroneously attributed to Marx. Schäffle, it should be noted, was writing in no hostile spirit ; his object was to get at the heart of Socialism and explain it as clearly as possible. Such was the confusion of thought enveloping the question that it took him years of study to disentangle the idea expressed above. The leaders of the international movement, he said, and especially Marx, were very cautious in enunciating their positive programme ; but 'every intelligent reader and logical thinker will recognise in the above statement the fundamental idea and aim of Socialism.'

I have introduced this reference here somewhat out of place, because the parallelism shows the continuity of thought between the first and second phases of Socialism, and the true place in the movement of the former, which has been unjustly

[1] *Quintessence of Socialism*, p. 3.

depreciated to increase the glory of the latter. As a matter of historical fact all the cardinal ideas and arguments brought forward in the second phase had been propounded in the first.

I pass on to the origin of the word 'Socialism.' This was coined independently in France a little later, about the year 1830. Its author was Pierre Leroux, who repeatedly declares that he invented the term, and whose claim was not disputed by contemporary writers.[1] Leroux was one of the most thoughtful and original writers of the period, and a very interesting figure.[2] He belonged to the Saint-Simonian school, to be described in the next chapter, but to the moderate, not to the more extravagant wing of it; and it was to the extreme views of the latter that he originally applied the word 'Socialism' in a disapproving sense. He protested against its general application to the whole school and particularly to his own views. Writing in 1850 he says:

'When I invented the term 'Socialism' as the

[1] Kirkup's statement that the word 'Socialism' was coined in England and borrowed from there by Reybaud, 'as he himself tells us in his well-known work *Réformateurs modernes*,' is a string of mistakes. It was not coined in England, Reybaud does not say that he borrowed it, nor is that the correct title of his book. What he says is that he had the unhappy honour of introducing the word *Socialist* into the French language.

[2] Pierre Leroux (1798–1871), born near Paris of an artisan family. The death of his father compelled him to go to work at an early age to support the family. Having worked first as a mason and later as a compositor he founded in 1830, with a partner, a daily newspaper named *Le Globe*, which through his instrumentality became at the beginning of 1831 the organ of the Saint-Simonian sect or church, as they called it, of Socialism. Leroux was one of the few early Socialists who had been a workman. He first, with his friend Jean Reynaud, pointed out the division of society into 'bourgeoisie' and 'proletariat' and so furnished Marx with the formula for the class-war, though Leroux himself did not preach it. See Chapter vii.

antithesis to "Individualism" I did not expect that twenty years later it would be applied in a general way to the religious democracy (the Saint-Simonian sect). What I attacked under that term were the false systems put forward by pretended disciples of Saint-Simon and of Rousseau.'[1]

He further explains that by 'Socialism' he meant 'the exaggerated expression of the idea of association or of society,' just as the term 'individualism,' which had come into use a few years before, meant the exaggerated expression of the idea of individual personality. He condemned both and sought to reconcile the social and individual elements by a middle course, which brought him the ridicule of the extreme Socialists. When the term, to his annoyance, became generally applied to all who, in any degree emphasised the social as against the individual element in human nature, he called the more extreme view 'absolute Socialism.' He realised, with perfect clearness, the complete antithesis of the two extremes and the evils of both.

'We are to-day,' he says, 'the prey of these two exclusive systems of Individualism and Socialism. . . . While the partisans of Individualism rejoice or console themselves over the ruins of Society and take refuge in their egoism, the partisans of Socialism, marching bravely towards what they call an organic epoch, are busy seeking how to bury all liberty, all spontaneity, beneath what they call organisation. . . . We are, then, between Charybdis and Scylla; between the theory of a government

[1] *Œuvres*, I. 161.

concentrating in itself all intelligence and all morality, and that of a government deprived by its own decree of both ; between an infallible pope on the one hand and a common gendarme on the other. The one party call their Individualism liberty and would fain give it the name of fraternity ; the others call their despotism a family. Heaven preserve us from a fraternity so little charitable and from a family so intrusive.'[1]

Again he refers to absolute Socialism as 'this new papacy, crushing, all-absorbing, which would transform humanity into a mechanism, in which the real, living creatures, the individuals, would be nothing but useful matter instead of being themselves the arbiters of their own destiny.'

These passages are from an essay on *Individualism and Socialism*, published in 1834, but an earlier use of the word in the same sense occurs in *Le Globe* of 13th February, 1832, in the course of a review of some poems by Victor Hugo, signed X. Joncieres, which may be a *nom de plume* of Leroux. At any rate, the sentiments are his : '*Nous ne voulons pas sacrifier la personalité au socialisme pas plus que ce dernier à la personalité*.' 'We do not wish to sacrifice personality to Socialism any more than to sacrifice the latter to personality.'

This early French conception of Socialism is not less striking than the English one. They are entirely different, but complementary to each other, the one abstract, broad and general, the other concrete, narrow and precise. Both hold good to-day. I have already shown that the replacement of private

[1] *Œuvres*, I. 375.

or public ownership of capital is the core of the thing as a concrete proposition, and always has been through all its changes of appearance. Regarded in the abstract and in relation to human nature this proposition is most certainly an extreme assertion of the social principle, and that conception has proved as lasting as the other. The criticism of Leroux that absolute Socialism would crush individuality and destroy liberty is precisely the great standing argument against it to-day. These two ideas are two threads which run unbroken, though often obscured, through the whole history of the movement. If one holds fast to them much of the confusion subsides, and it becomes possible to put subsidiary ideas in their proper places.

The one enables us to distinguish Socialism from other movements or influences, having something in common with it; from social reform, which is not concerned with the ownership of capital; from Communism, which is concerned with the ownership not only of capital, but of all property; from State action, which interferes with individual liberty in a thousand ways that have nothing to do with economic conditions; from Christianity, which is essentially concerned with individual conduct and spiritual life, not with the economic system. The other and broader definition shows us where Socialism stands in relation to civilisation in general, and to the problem of reconciling the social and individual principles in man, and so gives us a measure by which to judge its several forms and detailed applications. In so far as it corrects the excesses of individualism, it is beneficial; in so far as it suppresses individuality, it is pernicious.

Chapter II

THE FIRST PHASE OF SOCIALISM

England and France

I HAVE dwelt at some length on the origin of Socialism for the reasons given in the introduction, and also because it is generally ignored or erroneously described. The whole of the first phase of the movement is commonly set aside with a wave of the hand as 'Utopian,' in docile obedience to the dictum of Marx and Engels, who characteristically depreciated all their French and English predecessors and claimed the credit of discovering the only true Socialism—their own German brand.

We shall come to it in due course and examine those pretensions; but meanwhile I wish once more to emphasise the need for studying the beginnings of Socialism, if one is to understand it. I divide the whole movement into three phases or periods, and the first is the key to the rest. It was a time of ferment and extraordinarily fertile in ideas, called forth by the circumstances previously described; compared with it the later periods have been curiously sterile. The more one studies the early Socialists the more one is struck by their intellectual vigour. It was, indeed, too exuberant. It ran to waste and threw out fantastic growths, particularly in France; but it also produced all the live ideas that have animated the movement in its later stages. And behind this intellectual activity was a lofty enthusiasm, a spirit of benevolence. Voluntary co-operation was the dominant idea of the new order: the reconciliation of interests, not conflict, was its hope, at least until the period approached its close. There is to-day a tendency to do more justice to the early period, and to find in it the original expression of ideas which are now regaining ground. Even orthodox Marxian Socialists are becoming more appreciative. One of them writing in the *Socialist Encyclopædia* says of the early French Socialists, though not himself a Frenchman: 'In no country in this world do we find such an abundance of socialistic ideas and of original, brilliant or at least striking personalities, moved by a single desire to regenerate our old and sick society, as we do in France—the true cradle of Socialism, both of the Utopian and of the modern scientific type.'

In a book published in 1923 a French Socialist, Lucien Deslinières, quotes this passage and shows what a lively and sympathetic interest the movement then excited among men of mark. He goes on:

'Eighty years ago Socialism had penetrated into all quarters capable of thought: it was everywhere loved: everywhere its advent was desired. Why? Because it presented itself to the world under its reconstructive aspect, that is to say humane, benevolent, fraternal, full of promise for justice and happiness. To-day, apart from the advanced guard enrolled under the Marxian standard, it has aroused universal execration. Why? Because Marxism, a purely destructive doctrine, excludes every generous ideal and turns to ridicule the most natural sentiments of the human heart, because it constantly asserts itself by menace and violence, because the doctrine of the class war, without being itself based on hate, engenders hate by the inevitable interpretation it receives from labour; because, finally, it lends to Socialism the appearance of a party of disorder and subversion, totally incapable, not only of realising but even of conceiving a better society.'[1]

Now it is quite true that the movement in its early stages did attract wide and favourable attention, not only in France but even more, perhaps, in England. It was Lord Melbourne who in this period uttered the remark, subsequently repeated by Sir William Harcourt, "We are all Socialists now." A French judge said exactly the same thing at the trial of a Socialist brought before him. In both countries there were groups who pushed their theories to an extreme and entertained more revolutionary ideas; and their tendency grew towards the end of the period, when general political excitement prevailed. But broadly the character of Socialism in this period was peaceful, non-compulsory, benevolent and constructive; when it grew more revolutionary towards the stormy year 1848, it lost favour and excited hostility.

Though contemporary and mutually sympathetic, the movements in France and England presented

[1] *Délivrons-nous du Marxisme*, p. 13.

wide and characteristic differences. The greatest difference was that though the initiative in both countries was purely intellectual, the movement in England took a more practical turn and became associated with the organisation of labour almost from the beginning, whereas in France, where there was no such organisation, it remained mainly theoretical up to the experiment of national workshops in the revolution of 1848. The story in England is rather of attempts to do something on a comparatively simple basis of ideas; in France it is one of theories and plans poured out in extraordinary profusion and variety with little attempt to put them into execution.

It is not possible to tell either story here in detail, but at least an outline must be given, particularly of French Socialism, because there is no adequate account of it in our language, and in some respects it has more interest to-day, when there is a distinct tendency to revert to ideas then put forward by certain French writers. The English movement, on the other hand, has been described in great detail by Mr. Max Beer in his *History of British Socialism*; and an illuminating account of some of the principal writers is also given by Professor Foxwell in his introduction to the English version of Dr. Anton Menger's *Right to the Whole Produce of Labour,* as well as by Dr. Menger himself. Both these works can be unreservedly recommended.

The English Movement

To begin with the English movement, an erroneous impression has been created by confining attention too exclusively to Robert Owen.[1] It is corrected in the two works just mentioned, but still prevails. Owen's varied and ceaseless activities undoubtedly inspired other men and played an influential part in starting and sustaining the movement; and his reputation, gained as a philanthropic employer and social reformer, made it widely known. But he was no thinker and contributed nothing to the economic theory of Socialism. His philosophy of life was derived from Godwin's *Political Justice*, published in 1793, and rested on the ancient theory of determinism or denial of free will and responsibility. The argument is that human character is the result of heredity and environment, for neither of which is the individual responsible, and that all evil is due to bad environment and belief in the moral law taught by religion.

At the mature age of twelve, he tells us in his autobiography, he had thought the matter out and come to the conclusion that not only Christianity, but all religion, is essentially false and harmful. Starting from this standpoint, which he never abandoned, he developed his theory of a 'New

[1] Robert Owen (1771–1858), born at Newtown, N. Wales, the son of a small tradesman; when 10 years old was apprenticed to a draper at Stamford, at 20 became a cotton mill manager in Manchester, and afterwards a partner in a large mill in Scotland, where he introduced a benevolent system of control which attracted the attention of kings and statesmen; took up social reform ideas about 1817, when he presented a memorandum on the Poor Law to Parliament; started model settlements in Scotland and America in 1825, lost money, withdrew from Scottish mill in 1828, devoted himself to writing pamphlets, lecturing, debating and organising schemes.

Moral World,' in which all human ills would disappear and everyone be made good and happy by discarding the mischievous delusion of moral responsibility, the great misleader of mankind up till then, and replacing it by the right external circumstances. He expounded this theory in a series of essays published between 1813 and 1836, and was evidently quite unaware that the question of free will and moral responsibility was the subject of a very old philosophical controversy, settled once for all by Kant and summed up with masterly brevity by Dr. Johnson in the remark: "All theory is against the freedom of the will, all experience is for it." Owen's views have a modern interest because denial of individual responsibility and belief in external circumstances, to be provided by changing 'the system,' are implicit in all socialistic teaching. In 1906 Mr. Blatchford devoted a volume, entitled *Not Guilty,* to reproducing Owen's arguments.

But Owen did more than propound a theory; he had a plan for realising it. This was to establish model settlements on a voluntary co-operative basis, and in 1825 attempts were made to carry out the idea in Scotland and in America. Both experiments failed after a brief trial. Owen had further a vision of the great 'Co-operative Commonwealth,' of which we hear so much to-day, to be formed by federating the several settlements into a united whole. If this is Utopian, then the modern Co-operative Commonwealth is still more so. Owen and the men he inspired did at least make a start in the practical realisation of the plan by setting up the first units, whereas the present ideal is still in the air. The contemptuous dismissal of the first phase of Socialism as 'Utopian' has been too readily accepted from Marx and Engels. A Utopia is, properly speaking, a purely imaginary community, which has no existence, but is supposed to exist and is described as existing; that is the meaning of the word, which signifies 'Nowhere.' But the experiments were real and did exist for a time.

The English Socialism of this period was, in truth, less visionary and more practical than the later Marxian variety. If Utopian merely means ideal, the charge is true of the early Socialists, both English and French, but that is no condemnation; the latest tendency to-day, at least here, is to restore the ideal elements. Owen was himself always trying to do something; his mind was essentially constructive and he was opposed to all merely destructive tendencies. He was full of plans down to the end of his long life. Besides the model settlements just mentioned, he set up, in 1832, a labour exchange market in London, where producer and consumer were to be brought together without the intervention of middlemen, and goods were to be bought and sold without money, which was replaced by labour notes, representing equivalent quantities of labour on the theory, derived from Ricardo and subsequently made the basis of Marx's economic argument, that the true measure of value in goods is the quantity of labour embodied in them. This, too, failed after a very short run. Proposals to renew the experiment have been made again to-day.

None of Owen's schemes succeeded, but the influence of his personality and activity on other men was great, far-reaching and lasting. He commanded general attention in Europe and America, and enlisted the interest of politicians, reformers and economists; he stimulated the organisation of labour and planted the tree of co-operation, which has since borne fruit, though not the fruit he expected; and he inspired a number of writers who attacked the existing order on the economic side, and, more than any other school, gave Socialism an economic basis. The impulse which he imparted in these several ways was in most cases deflected before long into some different direction of which he disapproved, and he was constantly at variance with his own disciples who kept breaking away; but he was none the less a motive force.

The widest influence he exercised had to do with social reform, not Socialism, and took effect in promoting factory legislation and popular education. But the organisations formed under his inspiration had a strong infusion of Socialism or Communism, and they were fertile soil for the growth of ideas; some ideas which then first found expression were revived long afterwards and thought to be new, for instance, internationalism, the general strike, syndicalism, the motto 'Each for All and All for Each.' Mention has already been made of the London Co-operative Society, founded in 1824, and of the term 'Socialist' coined in the course of its discussions. It was formed to promote the principles of mutual co-operation, with the object of restoring 'the whole produce of labour to the labourer.' The influence of William Thompson (see below) is here apparent It seems to have been mainly an intellectual society, as I have already said, and to have lasted until 1830.

Of more importance was the 'National Union of the Working Classes,' founded in 1831, when trade unionism, which had been emancipated in 1824, was growing in strength. This organisation brought workmen into the movement and signalised a new departure; the older Owenite campaign was at first reinforced and then superseded by trade unionism and political agitation. It is an interesting coincidence that the same year witnessed a great labour demonstration in France, where trade unions were prohibited, in the violent rising of the Lyons weavers, which gave a fresh impetus to the Socialist movement.

It was a time of general excitement. There had been a political revolution in France in 1830, and in England agitation for electoral reform was rising rapidly. The National Union, which adopted the motto 'Each for All, and All for Each,' took up the agitation for the Reform Bill and became a confused medley of Socialism, Trade Unionism and Radical politics, with a growing revolutionary bent. International action and the general strike were both propounded at National Union meetings in 1831. After the passage of the Reform Bill in 1832 this triple division became accentuated and the movement split up. The political agitation began to develop into Chartism, while the trade union movement turned away towards direct action, and under the influence of Morrison and Smith, who took the lead and developed the syndicalist idea of ousting capitalist employers and replacing them by the organised workmen in each industry. Between the two, Socialism fell to the ground; the end disappeared and was smothered by the means.

The trade union movement was the first to collapse after a brief spell of delirious excitement. It grew with fabulous rapidity in 1833, but it was a fungus growth. In 1834 the modern syndicalist idea of 'Greater Unionism' or 'One Big Union' was anticipated by the formation of the 'Grand National Consolidated Trades Union,' but it was still-born, and revolutionary trade unionism collapsed. This stimulated the political movement which went on in the form of Chartism, so called from the Charter, a demand for adult male suffrage, equal electoral districts, secret ballots, annual Parliaments and payment of members. These measures were at first intended by some of the leading Chartists as a means to the furtherance of Socialism, though that gradually dropped out of sight. The movement had a constitutional and an unconstitutional side and was eventually wrecked by the latter in 1848. The chief working-class leader and the most earnest man in the movement, William Lovett, who drafted the Charter, changed his views later and warned his fellow-workmen against 'vain theories, impracticable measures and empty threats or denunciations.'[1]

The economic theory that lay behind all these movements and gave them logical support was furnished by a number of intellectual writers, who took up the cause under the influence of Owen's example, but did their own thinking. The most

[1] See p. 83.

important of them was William Thompson.[1] His standpoint is thus stated in the Preliminary Observations to his book on Wealth, written in 1822:

> 'The tendency of the existing arrangement of things as to wealth is to enrich a few at the expense of the mass of the producers; to make the poverty of the poor more hopeless, to throw back the middling classes upon the poor, that a few may be enabled not only to accumulate in perniciously large masses the real national, which is only the aggregate of individual, capital, but also by means of such accumulations to command the products of the yearly labour of the community.'[2]

It will be seen that he closely follows Sismondi, and his explanation of the disparity is the same. The labourer by his work on the material creates surplus value which is taken by the capitalist. 'In the usual course of things the productive labourer is deprived of at least half the products of his labour by the capitalist.'[3] The evil is due to the divorce of the labourer from the ownership of capital, and the remedy lies in re-uniting them.

> 'It is as inconsistent with human happiness in general, as with the greatest production of

[1] William Thompson (1780?–1833), Irish landowner, originally influenced by the Utilitarianism of Bentham, converted to Socialism by observing ill effects of existing economic order; published in 1824 *An Inquiry into the Principles of the Distribution of Wealth most conducive to Human Happiness; applied to the newly proposed system of 'voluntary equality of wealth.'*

[2] *Inquiry, etc.*, p. xvi.

[3] *Inquiry, etc.*, p. 166.

wealth, that capital should be possessed by one set of individuals and labour by another ; utility demands that all productive labourers should become capitalists, that labour and capital should be in the same hands.'[1]

This is extremely interesting in view of the most recent tendencies. Thompson's remedy was the voluntary co-operative system with common ownership of capital as advocated by the London Co-operative Society and stated in the first definition of 'Socialist' quoted in the previous chapter ; but obviously there is another way by which labourers can become capitalists, namely, by being taken into partnership. This has often been proposed and attempted, so far with chequered success ; but it has been much more successful than Owen's co-operative communities or any other alternative method of realising the same ideal yet tried, and it is far from being abandoned. The very latest movements, which have originated in America and are referred to in the last chapter of this book, show the vitality of the idea and its adaptability.

It is not necessary to enter into the views of the other economic Socialists who followed Thompson—Hodgskin, Gray, Minter Morgan, Edmonds, Ravenstone and Bray ; they are only variants of the same fundamental theme, and full accounts of them are given by Mr. Beer and Professor Foxwell in the books already mentioned.

[1] *Inquiry, etc.*, p. 590.

The Movement in France

Two names are always mentioned as corresponding in France to Robert Owen in England. These are Saint-Simon and Fourier. They resembled Owen in that they inspired disciples who formed schools of thought and propaganda; but they started no schemes and carried on no agitation as he did. In the later stages of this first phase of Socialism, which covered just the same period in France as in England, other schools and other leaders arose and the field became a welter of diverse and conflicting opinions.

The Saint-Simonian school first occupied the field, though Fourier's principal work had been published some years before Saint-Simon began to write on subjects bearing on Socialism. Fourier, however, had no followers for more than twenty years and his ideas were not taken up until after the stirring events of 1830–31. Meanwhile a society of disciples had been formed just before the death of Saint-Simon in 1825, as stated in Chapter I, to carry on his teaching, and they published, posthumously, his last and most important work, *The New Christianity.*[1] Science, industry and religion were the keynotes of his philosophy, which had for its aim the reorganisation of society in the interests of

[1] Claude Henri de Rouvroy, Comte de Saint-Simon (1760–1824) born in Paris of an ancient and aristocratic family, descended from Charlemagne; studied science under D'Alembert, assisted in the revolt of the American colonies, projected a Panama Canal and other large schemes; took no part in the Revolution, cherished the ambition of founding a high school of science and a great industrial establishment; lost all his money and fell into great poverty; published *Letters from a Resident in Geneva*, a political work, in 1802; a scheme for a United States of Europe in 1814; a book on *Industry* in 1817, *The Organizer* 1819-20, *The Industrial System* 1821-22, *The New Christianity*, posthumously in 1825.

the poorer classes. 'Religion,' he declared, 'ought to direct society towards the great aim of ameliorating as speedily as possible the lot of the most numerous and poorest class.' This was the immediate object, which he regarded as a necessary step towards the larger aim of the universal association of mankind, in accordance with the theory of social evolution which was his interpretation of history. He held that history showed us mankind tending always to association on a higher scale—the family, the city, the nation, the federation of nations—by a series of stages, each containing the germ of the next one and leading to it by a logical process. In the final stage strife within and between societies will cease and all be harmoniously combined.

This conception of social evolution anticipates the Marxian theory, which was the basis of 'Scientific Socialism,' and it is more consonant with the facts of history than the hypothesis of the class war. Saint-Simon emphatically repudiated the use of force and relied on persuasion. The immediate social improvement he aimed at—the raising of the poorest section of the population—was to be secured by a re-organisation of the economic order under the guidance of scientific men, artists and industrialists penetrated by the true spirit of Christianity, which had been perverted and obscured. Thus religion, knowledge and industry were to be united and together create a new order organised hierarchically, but for the peaceful administration of affairs, not the forcible government of men. This distinction has been recently revived by M. Vandervelde; it coincides with and anticipates the idea of the 'withering away' of the State, as an organ of authority, propounded by Marx and Engels.

Saint-Simon's ideas, sketched by him in broad outline and presented in the form of open letters and dialogues, were taken up energetically and elaborated after his death by his disciples, who formed a veritable, though far from harmonious, school. It included many men of marked ability, who afterwards became famous in one way or another. Among the most prominent disciples were Comte, Halevy, Blanqui, Enfantin, Bazard, Rodrigues, Buchez, Chevalier, Carnot, Péreire, Leroux, and Reynaud. They held no well-defined and agreed body of doctrine, but according to the authoritative statement presented to the Chamber of Deputies in 1830 by Bazard and Enfantin the main tenets of the school were these: they laid great stress on the distinction between the idle and industrious, between earned and unearned income; their motto was, 'From each according to his capacity, to each according to his works.' They recognised natural inequality as an indispensable basis of association; they repudiated communism and the equal distribution of goods, and would give to each member of society what he earned; they maintained the rights of property, but would gradually eliminate unearned income by abolishing inheritance, and in this way transfer by degrees the means of production, land and capital from private hands to the new social authority, so that no one should live in idleness on the labour of others. They advocated the complete emancipation of women.

This policy has an uncommonly modern ring,

and when it was formulated in 1831 it attracted many fresh adherents among men of letters, artists, philosophers and industrials. It became fashionable, like Owenism in England and Labourism to-day. But almost from the first divisions had appeared in the school, which soon began to split up, as indicated by the extracts from Pierre Leroux given in the last chapter. Then public scandal was created by the proceedings of the extreme wing led by Enfantin, who under cover of religion took up free love and general bodily indulgence. This led to a prosecution and the imprisonment of Enfantin in 1832, which brought discredit on the whole sect and destroyed its influence, though individual members continued to profess and propagate the doctrine. The tendency of ardent regenerators of society to run to free love is a curious phenomenon not sufficiently noticed; a desire to indulge their appetites seems bound up with their objections to the existing order, which imposes more restraint than they like.

After the collapse of the Saint-Simonian school and the dispersion of its members, the torch was carried on by another group inspired by the theories of Fourier.[1] He was a deeper thinker than either Saint-Simon or Owen and went further back to first principles, but he was moved by the same

[1] Francois Charles Marie Fourier (1772–1837), born at Besançon, the son of a well-to-do draper; was early disgusted by the trickery of commerce; lost the fortune left by his father in the Revolution; lived subsequently in poverty; was well educated and studied assiduously, an original and independent thinker with a tendency to mysticism; in 1803 published an article on European politics which attracted great attention; in 1808 published his *Theory of the Four Movements*, which excited nothing but ridicule at the time; his later works were a treatise on Association, 1822, *The New Industrial World*, 1828, an attack on Saint-Simon and Owen, 1831, and numerous articles.

impulse—profound dissatisfaction with the existing order and the competition and strife accompanying it. Like them he stressed the principle of association as the remedy, but had his own plan for realising it. This so far resembled Owen's that it consisted in organising society in small separate communities called phalanxes, the members of which were to carry on all economic operat ons in association. Their functions were to be minu organised on a scientific plan resting on the principle of attraction, which assured the combination of liberty with association.

In working out his theory of attraction Fourier passed into an obscure region of thought, which seemed merely ridiculous to his contemporaries, but has a certain affinity to modern philosophical speculation, while the functional basis of his industrial organisation, which was to produce perfect social harmony, anticipates an idea much in favour to-day. In another point also Fourier anticipated some modern tendencies of economic thought. In his phalanxes, the wealth produced by the community was first to furnish every member with adequate maintenance, and then the surplus was to be divided in fixed proportion between labour (five-twelfths), capital (four-twelfths), and talent (three-twelfths). This was a bold attempt to solve a problem that still puzzles economists, and the recognition of talent (now generally called brains or ability) as entitled to a share reveals a clear insight into the real conditions of production. Fourier, like the Saint-Simonians, but still more decidedly, recognised inequality and private property. Finally his phalanxes, like Owen's co-operative communities were to be federated into a world union. If Owen did not derive any of his ideas from Fourier, the points of resemblance form a remarkable coincidence. Several attempts made by Fourier's disciples to found phalanxes in France, Algeria, America and Brazil failed as completely as the Owenite communities.

A knowledge of the doctrines of Fourier and Saint-Simon as pioneers of Socialism in France is indispensable to a student of the movement; but they can no more be regarded as covering the field than Owen in England. They set the ball rolling, but it was taken up later and tossed hither and thither by other hands in a wild game of competitive theory-making, in which old pupils of the original schools struck out in new directions and new men arose with fresh ideas. To give a detailed account of them is neither possible in a limited space nor necessary for the present purpose; but the most prominent figures and their views must be noticed because they led up to the second or Marxian phase of Socialism. They were much younger men than the three pioneers, of whom it is to be observed that they were all past middle age when they took Socialistic ideas, which goes to confirm the view that Socialism was a post-Waterloo phenomenon, called into existence by the extraordinary conditions then prevailing.

To understand the developments in France, with which we are dealing, it is necessary to remember that from 1830 onwards Europe in general, and France in particular, were in a state of agitation, varying in intensity, but continuous and tending to increase. We have already noted the ferment in England beginning in 1830 and marked by the meteoric rise of labour organisations with strong Socialistic tendencies, which later were turned into the long political agitation called Chartism. In France kindred forces were at work and naturally assumed a more revolutionary colour in a country where revolution had become a habit of mind. In 1830 the ferment produced a constitutional revolution, resulting in the abdication of Charles X and the accession of Louis Philippe to the throne. It was a democratic change, like the Reform Act of 1832 in England; but far more significant than any political move was the rising of Lyons weavers in 1831, when the National Union of the Working Classes was getting into its stride in England. It was the first entry on the stage of the 'proletariat.' They were wholly unorganised, but driven to desperation by the hopelessness of their situation. There is an axiom, much in favour with agitators who have to explain the inconsistency of popular apathy with the misery they continually declare to exist, that misery does not excite to revolt, but merely crushes. All history is against them, and the Lyons weavers are a case in point. Proudhon stated the truth when he said that revolutions were caused not so much by the distress felt at the moment as by its prolongation and the hopelessness engendered by the tendency of conditions to get worse. The silk-weavers of Lyons numbered from 30,000 to 40,000, and their earnings had dropped from 3*s.* 4*d.* to 1*s.* 3*d.* a day, in some cases to 9*d.* for 18 hours' work; nor was there any hope of improvement. They demanded a minimum living wage, which was refused by the 'little masters' who employed them. They rose in arms and descended on Lyons from the Croix Rousse, their own quarter. The National Guard failed to disperse them, the prefect of the Rhone Department and the military fled, and the weavers were left in possession of the field. The incident marked the beginning of a long period of industrial disturbance and revolutionary agitation. In 1834 the Lyons weavers again rose and fought a pitched battle with the military, lasting five days; artillery was used, and 1,200 persons killed. This was the most serious episode, but there were many others; and at the same time on the political side many secret revolutionary and republican societies were formed. The great agitator in this sphere was Blanqui.

This period of violent disturbance, which did not come to an end till 1839, moved the younger Socialists to activity in the search for a way out. The most noteworthy of them were Considérant, Louis Blanc, Pecqueur, Cabet and Proudhon.

Victor Considérant (1808–1893) was an engineer officer in the Army, who was attracted by the doctrines of Fourier and resigned his commission in 1831 in order to propagate them. Up till then Fourier had had only one disciple, Just Muiron. Considérant published in 1835 the first of a long series of works advocating Fourierism, and became the head of the school, to which he remained faithful. He strongly combated Communism and maintained that abolition of private property was impossible without civil war, in which he anticipated Lenin. (Russia has also proved the truth of his statement that the peasant is invulnerable to Communism.) His interpretation of history agreed with Lord Acton's; he saw in it since the advent of Christianity a continual advance of liberty in three stages: (1) from slavery to serfdom (2) from serfdom to wage-earning, which was industrial feudalism, (3) from wage-earning to partnership, the last step being the problem of the age, to be solved by the Fourier system. It has emerged again to-day.

Louis Blanc (1811–1882) was the son of a high official and well educated. He studied law, became a journalist and took up Socialism, in which he broke new ground. In 1840 he published in a Socialist review his famous essay on the *Organisation of Labour*. He started, like all the rest, with the evils of the existing competitive system, which he declared to be a system of extermination for the people and a perpetual cause of impoverishment and ruin for the employers. He proved the first proposition by statistics of wages and cost of living in quite a modern manner; the second by the effects on the market, the chaotic disorder, commercial scandals and the example of England. It must, he said, entail war between England and France. This is interesting because capitalism is now said to be the sole cause of war, and he thought it inevitable eighty-four years ago; but that war has not come yet. He drew the inference that it was to everyone's interest to get rid of the system. How? By bringing in the power of the State, which was to squeeze out private employers by setting up social workshops and furnishing tools to the workmen, who after the first year would be able to run the shops themselves—a neat combination of State Socialism and Syndicalism, almost identical with Guild Socialism.

It was Louis Blanc who first formulated the motto, 'To each according to his needs and from each according to his capacity;' which shows how far Socialism had travelled from the Saint-Simonian standpoint. He also formulated the famous 'Right to Work,' which was taken up here as a militant slogan after the war. In 1848 he became a member of the provisional government after the Revolution of that year, and since unemployment was severe he had an opportunity of putting the right to work or maintenance into practice. This was done in Paris, not by social workshops, but by relief works of the ordinary kind. The men were paid two francs a day, but since it was impossible to find work for all the unemployed, the rest received a maintenance dole of one and a half francs. The result was that the men on the works did as little as possible. They openly argued that since the Government gave them twenty pence a day for working and fifteen pence for not working, their work was worth only five pence a day, and they need do no more. Eventually the whole thing was swamped by numbers, which ran up to 100,000 representing 187 occupations, and came to an end in bloodshed. No more was heard of the right to work in France. It is often said that this was not a fair trial of the national workshops' scheme, and of course it was not, but a trial was made of the plan in special workshops for tailors and bootmakers, which were also unsuccessful. Meanwhile, other and more extreme forms of Socialism had been brought forward.

Constantin Pecqueur (1801–1851) carried the idea of State action farther than Louis Blanc and advocated the full Collectivism that was so long the dominant type of Socialism in the second phase. He must be regarded as the father of that doctrine. He began as a Saint-Simonian much in accord with Leroux; but he had his own ideas and gradually went to the extreme condemned by Leroux. He was a prolific contributor to the numerous journals then run by French Socialists, and in 1842 he published *A New Theory of Social and Political Economy*, which contained a *résumé* of his ideas. He maintained that property and the method of production should be completely transformed. Individual ownership should be suppressed, capital of all kinds should be socialised and production should be carried on by the State. This was the only way to escape from industrial feudalism—quite the modern standpoint.

Etienne Cabet (1788–1856) represented more completely than any other contemporary the return to the much older idea of Communism, towards which a strong tendency manifested itself at this time. He was an older man than the others mentioned above and one of strongly marked character. Though the son of a working cooper he educated himself for the bar and in 1831 was returned to the Chamber of Deputies, where he made such violent attacks on the Government that in 1834 he had to leave France. He took refuge in England where he read More's Utopia and interested himself in Owen's plans. This experience, which lasted till 1839, turned him into a real Utopian after the manner of Sir Thomas More. His *Travels in Icaria*, published in 1840, described an imaginary country, the inhabitants of which lived under a completely communistic system. This lengthy romance—Considérant speaks of his 'great and loquacious activity'—was much read by French workmen and had no small influence among them. But Cabet, unlike Sir Thomas More, was not content with an allegory; he urged the adoption of Icarian principles, which were reduced to a more precise statement in another work, *The Communist Credo.* In 1848 he followed the example of Owen, and established an Icarian settlement in Texas. At first they fared no better than Martin Chuzzlewit, having been beguiled into buying land which might have served Dickens—perhaps it did—as a model for Eden; so Cabet transferred his colony to a deserted Mormon town in Illinois. There the usual thing happened; quarrels broke out and Cabet assumed a dictatorship. He could no more stand opposition than Owen and after a few years was expelled by his dissatisfied subjects. The story closely resembles that of William Lane and New Australia some forty years later.

But the most interesting figure among all the men of that time was Proudhon.[1] Though of humble birth he was the most prolific, vigorous, original and independent writer during the first phase of the Socialist movement, and more than any other he prepared the way for Marx and the second phase. He belonged to no school, but criticised them all impartially and stood alone, the best hated and most abused man in France, as he

[1] Pierre Joseph Proudhon (1809–1865), like Fourier, a native of Besançon, son of an artisan, became a compositor, like Leroux, and then took to literary study and writing; in 1840 published his most famous work, *What is Property?* in 1846 published the book on *Economic Contradictions or the Philosophy of Misery*, which drew on him a bitter attack by Marx, because he condemned Communism, which Marx then favoured. Proudhon continued to write and expand his theories after the collapse of 1848, and his influence lingered into the second phase, when for several years it competed in France with that of Marx.

says himself. This was because his early utterances seemed outrageous and he was thought a dangerous character. His first published work was the celebrated essay *What is Property?* to which his answer was, 'Property is theft.' The sentiment was not new. Locke, writing of the origin of property, says that a man who took and laid up more than his share of what Nature provided—that is, more than he could use—'robbed others,' and later writers about the time of the French Revolution applied the word theft to the same proceeding; but no one had argued the question at such length and with so much force or had laid it down in such uncompromising terms that all property is theft. Proudhon himself did not mean it so and afterwards modified the statement, but it has stuck to him ever since. What he meant was what Sismondi and Thompson had already said and Marx repeated later, namely that the workman was robbed by the capitalist, who paid him enough for subsistence and pocketed the rest. His second title to fame is that he was the father of Anarchism. He condemned State Collectivism, and, taking up the mantle of Saint-Simon, argued on historical and economic grounds that what would happen in the future was that industrial organisation would take the place of government in the old sense, and that the State as the organ of authority would disappear, since there would be no need of it. But he did not preach Anarchism as a policy and was, in fact, as opposed to all destructive action as the other leading Socialists of his time; Marx accused him of wishing to reconcile the bourgeoisie and proletariat, which meant that he looked to peaceful methods. He pointed out, not only the effect of modern industry on the workman, in which he followed Sismondi, but also the contradiction between social production and individual distribution, on which so much stress is laid to-day.

Proudhon has been much misunderstood and accused of inconsistency through failure to understand his method, which was the posing of contradictory propositions after the manner of Kant, whom he held to be the greatest of philosophers. He was, said Considérant, the man of pure logic, weighing everything in the scales against its opposite. This method he applied in his *General Idea of the Revolution of the Nineteenth Century* to the interpretation of history put forward by Saint-Simon, whom alone he never attacked ; and if these features make Socialism scientific then his version is entitled to the epithet. His one practical proposal was the provision of gratuitous credit by a national bank, which would have the effect of abolishing interest on loaned capital.[1]

[1] His relations with Marx are of interest. They met in Paris in 1844 and found a good deal in common. Marx was attracted by his essay on Property, which he called ' epoch-making,' because it attacked the economic basis of civilisation, and they had long discussions, often lasting all night, according to Marx, who says that he " infected Proudhon with Hegelianism, much to his harm." After Marx's expulsion from Paris the education of Proudhon in German philosophy was continued by Karl Grün, who had, says Marx, " this advantage over me that he understood nothing of it himself." (Of course, nobody understood it or anything else but Marx himself, in the opinion of that modest thinker.) What turned him against Proudhon was the fact that the latter would not draw what Marx thought the logical (revolutionary) consequences of his own propositions, but proceeded to reconcile them, which meant a peaceful solution of social problems. Proudhon was not, in fact, infected with Marx's version of Hegel, but stuck to the method of Kant. Hence Marx's ferocious and wounding attack, which put an end to all intercourse, although Proudhon had made the most broad-minded offer of collaboration on the principle of bear and forbear or agreeing to differ.

CHAPTER III

THE SECOND PHASE

GERMANY

THE first phase of Socialism may be said to have closed with the revolutionary years 1848, which witnessed the establishment of the Second Republic in France and the collapse of Chartism in England. After that it declined as an active movement and fell into abeyance for many years, though French Socialists continued to write about it. But, before the curtain fell in the last act, there appeared for a moment on the stage the man whose personality was destined to dominate the second phase, in which the centre of gravity shifted to Germany. This was Marx,[1] who, in 1848, issued the famous Communist Manifesto, which he had drawn up in

[1] Karl Marx (1818–1883), born at Trier (Treves) in the Rhine province of Prussia, of a middle-class Christianised Jewish family. High school and university education; studied philosophy and contemplated an academic career, but his views were too advanced for the authorities; took up journalism in Cologne as an extreme Radical; compelled to leave Prussia and went to Paris in 1843; met there French Socialists, exiled German revolutionaries and Engels; expelled from France, went to Brussels in 1845, joined the League of the Just, a secret German Communist Society; published in 1847 his *Misère de la Philosophie*, an attack on Proudhon, in 1848 the Communist Manifesto; returned to Germany to join the revolution there, met Lassalle; went to London in 1849; published *Critique of Political Economy* in 1859 and 1st volume of *Das Kapital* in 1867. A story is current that he attended in boyhood a Jesuit school, from which he was expelled, but there were none in Germany at that time. The school he attended was the local 'gymnasium' or grammar school, and from which he was expelled, but it was locally called the Jesuit School, because it had formerly been occupied by that Society.

collaboration with Engels[1] for the Communist League, a secret international and revolutionary society formed, mainly under Marx's influence, out of the 'League of the Just,' which was the most important of several secret societies carried on by German revolutionary exiles in Paris, Switzerland and Brussels during the previous fifteen years. Marx, who even then claimed intellectual superiority and assumed the domineering attitude he maintained all his life, got hold of the League of the Just and converted it to his purpose, which was to proclaim the class war. It is worthy of note that in the transformation the old motto of the League, 'All men are Brothers,' was superseded by the international call to arms in the class war. This newcomer in the field not only ridiculed the French and English Socialists, whose ideas he annexed, but found even German revolutionary Communists too tame for his taste.

Neither he nor the Communist Manifesto, however, exercised any influence over the course of events at the time, or for many years after; and no more will be said of them for the present. But the gesture falls into place in the narrative here,

[1] Fredrich Engels (1820–1895), born at Barmen in the Rhine Province, father a well-to-do cotton manufacturer; high school education; entered the mill at 17 years of age; in 1838 went to Bremen to continue his business education, and in 1842 to Manchester, where the firm had a mill; on the way through Cologne made the acquaintance of Marx, then editing a Radical paper; in England met English Socialists and studied the Chartist movement; in 1844 returned to Germany, and in 1845 published his book on *The State of the Working Class in England*; had then met Marx again in Paris; collaborated with him in Brussels on the Communist Manifesto in 1847; took an active part in the German revolutionary insurrection in 1848; returned to England and re-entered the Manchester business in 1850; in 1877 published his book against Eugen Dühring, dealing with 'Utopian' and 'scientific' Socialism; in 1885 published posthumously Vol. II of Marx's *Kapital*, and in 1894, Vol. III. (The fourth and last volume was published by Kautsky in 1905–1910.)

as a connecting link between the first phase, from which it emanated, and the second, which it foreshadowed. The only active movement carried on in the interval between the two was the so-called Christian Socialism, which was not Socialism in the proper sense of the word, so much as the advocacy of social reform on Christian principles, or the application of Christian principles to current social problems with a strong infusion of democratic politics.

It arose out of the general turmoil that culminated in 1848 and it was carried on both in France and England by clerical and lay supporters in association. In France the post–1848 movement was not altogether new, having been preceded by an earlier one, rather political than social, led by Lamennais, whose Book of the People was published in 1837, and by Lacordaire. In England the appearance of Christian Socialism was signalised by Charles Kingsley's weekly paper, *Politics for the People*, which ran for seventeen numbers from 6th May to the end of July 1848. In Germany the movement, led by von Ketteler, bishop of Mainz, did not become active until considerably later. The attitude of the Churches and of individual churchmen towards the questions raised by Socialism is, however, a separate subject, which is discussed in a later chapter. The early movement just alluded to calls for mention only as an episode falling between the first and second phases of Socialism proper, and furnishing evidence of the sympathetic interest aroused by the former in religious circles. It did not last long, and had no connection with the second phase, to which we now come.

We get a definite starting point in the year 1863,

which the German Social Democratic Party named as the date of their foundation. In 1913 they celebrated their Jubilee; and since that was the year before the War, which broke up the movement, as it then was, into fragments and ushered in a new era, we may regard the whole phase as having lasted for fifty years or about twice as long as the first.

The differences between the two are numerous and great. The first phase had been confined as a movement to France and England, though it attracted attention in other countries; the second was international, but led by Germans and dominated throughout by German influence, with a strong Jewish element, which had been conspicuously absent in the first phase. In the second place the spirit was totally different; benevolence was superseded by bitterness, the motive of sympathy with the poor was overshadowed by hatred of the rich, the idea of co-operation was replaced by conflict, the voluntary principle by the compulsory, persuasion by aggression, aspiration and sentiment by hard-and-fast determination. Intellectually, free speculation gave place to rigid dogma, religious or ethical influences to pure materialism. In purpose, constructive aims were superseded by destructive ones, the improvement of existing conditions by their total abolition; in methods, the idea of force was introduced, and for gradual and evolutionary change more or less sudden and revolutionary action was substituted. These differences were summed up in the doctrine of the class-war, and they apply to the movement as a whole.

At the same time, conditions were also very different. Industry and trade had undergone a great expansion; wealth and population had grown with them; the state of extreme and general distress, out of which Socialism originally sprang, had passed away, and comparative prosperity prevailed. The troubles connected with the introduction of machinery had ceased; wages, both nominal and real, had risen; hours of work had been reduced. Life was easier all round. These and other material changes varied in different countries, but were most marked in England, which had furnished all the classical descriptions of the misery of the people in the earlier period. In England, too, there had been other changes—the progressive restriction of free enterprise and competition by factory laws and regulations, and the restraint exercised on employers by combination among the employed. Germany, though developing industrially, was in a backward position in all these respects, and this is, perhaps, one reason why the revival of Socialism began there, reached this country many years later, and made very slow progress when it did come.

However this may be, Germany was the seat of the new movement, which was primarily political, though the eventual object was economic. In this respect it may be said to have started where the old left off. The founder was not Marx, but Lassalle,[1] whose personal activity was prematurely cut short by a duel in 1864, but whose influence persisted

[1] Ferdinand Lassalle (1825–1864), born at Breslau of a well-to-do commercial Jewish family; had a high school and university education and also went for a short time to the school of commerce in Leipzig, but had no taste for business; took up the study of philosophy, history and literature; became a Socialist when only eighteen, mainly because of the harsh treatment of Jews, but came later under the influence of French Socialists during a visit to Paris; threw himself with ardour into the German revolutionary movement in 1848, which

for years afterwards. Lassalle owed little or nothing to Marx, but drew his inspiration direct from French sources, as did all revolutionary Germans of that period; Paris was to them the Mecca of liberty. He was most influenced by Louis Blanc and aimed at the organisation of Labour with State aid. He opened his campaign in 1862 with an address given to a meeting of workmen in Berlin, in which he outlined the idea, already made familiar by French writers, of raising the working classes to be the dominant power, as the next step in the historical evolution of society. This discourse was afterwards published as the Labour Programme and attracted more attention from the Government than from the workmen; Lassalle was prosecuted, but escaped with a small fine.

German workmen were at this time taking an interest in politics and in cultural improvement. For the former they looked to the Liberals; for the latter to the mutual improvement societies or institutes of which many had been formed. But they were not interested in economics and knew nothing of Socialism. Saxony was industrially the most highly developed part of Germany, and Leipzig the centre. Bebel, who was right in the middle of it (see below), says in his autobiography that Socialism and Communism meant nothing to them. They had not read the Communist Manifesto

brought him in contact with Marx, who visited Germany at that time; Lassalle was prosecuted and sentenced to six months imprisonment. In 1862 he entered the regular political field, with a view to forming a Labour or Democratic Party. A man of brilliant abilities and great learning, he commanded the admiration of Bismarck, but he was also a social butterfly, and threw away his life before he was forty in a duel on account of a love affair. He is the hero of George Meredith's novel *The Tragic Comedians*.

or the writings of other German Socialists and Communists—Wilhelm Weitling, Moses Hess,[1] Karl Grün, Karl Robertus and others—and took so little interest in such questions that a proposal made at the Congress of Workmen's Societies in 1863 to establish classes in economics and political theory was rejected—an instructive contrast to modern developments. But the German workmen were beginning to stir on their own account in a different way. If the intellectual leaders drew inspiration from France, the workmen looked rather to England and the trade union movement, which had developed there quite independently of Socialism. In 1862 a party of twelve German workmen were sent from Berlin by the National Society to visit the Exhibition in London, where they met fellow-workmen, and in this episode originated the idea of international organisation afterwards exploited by Marx.

The report of the German workmen on their return to Berlin led to the decision in agreement with the Leipzig Central Committee to hold a German Labour Congress at Leipzig; and Lassalle was invited to publish his views in a pamphlet, which he did in March 1863. The appearance of this document, which was entitled *Open Reply to the Central Committee*, was followed by the formation in May of the 'General German Workmen's Union,' which is regarded as the foundation of the Social Democratic Party, or organised Socialism in Germany, from which in turn sprang the revival of Socialism in other countries.

[1] Moses Hess, the most important of these, has been called the father of German Socialism, not without reason. He exercised a strong intellectual influence on both Marx and Lassalle and was, like them, of Jewish family.

The *Open Reply* began by declaring that the Radical or Progressive Party, on which the working classes had relied, had proved totally incapable of realising their aspirations and that they must form an independent party of their own, with the demand for universal, equal and direct suffrage as the main plank in their programme ; their policy should be a peaceful and constitutional agitation conducted by all lawful means. With regard to social questions, the co-operative and self-help institutions founded by Schulze of Delitsch on the English model, were welcomed and commended, but declared quite inadequate to effect any real improvement in the condition of the great bulk of workmen employed in the large industry. To prove this Lassalle expounded the famous 'brazen law of wages,' which is that under modern conditions and the control of supply and demand the average wage is always limited to the bare subsistence level required for the maintenance and propagation of life according to the customary standard of the nation. It is merely a variant of the observation originally made by Sismondi and repeated by others that competition forces workmen down to 'what is absolutely necessary for daily subsistence,' and that the orthodox theory of economics 'reduces the working class to the strictest necessaries.' The orthodox theory referred to was Ricardo's political economy, which furnished the basis of all the economic theories of Socialism from William Thompson to the Erfurt Programme. The brazen law has long been given up as a mistake by all educated Socialists, but it still figures implicitly or explicitly in propaganda.

So the ship was launched, and the first thing that happened was the inevitable outbreak of squabbling among the crew, which was not lessened by the death of the captain. Among his lieutenants the ablest man was J. B. Schweitzer, a barrister and a very clever manager who eventually became the leader of the Lassalleans. He endeavoured to enlist the co-operation of Marx and Engels, then in London, and offered the leadership to Marx, who declined it. However, one of his disciples did come in to assist in the new paper, the *Sozialdemokrat*, which was to be the organ of the party. This was Wilhelm Liebknecht,[1] who was destined to play an important part in future developments with Bebel.[2] The two came together in 1865, when

[1] William Liebknecht (1826–1900), born at Giessen of a middle-class family; had a high school and university education; fell under the influence of French Socialism; was expelled from Berlin and took refuge in Switzerland; flung himself into the revolutionary movement in 1848 and proclaimed a republic in Baden; after the collapse came to London, where he lived by teaching and writing for thirteen years in close contact with Marx; returned to Germany to edit an important North German paper in 1862, but soon gave it up. Joined the Lassalleans in 1864, but left them and joined Bebel in Leipzig in 1865; was elected to the North German Parliament in 1867, and to the Reichstag later; was joint leader of the Parliamentary Socialists with Bebel; became editor of the chief Socialist paper *Vorwärts*, in 1890; was a consistent follower of Marx and an uncompromising revolutionary.

[2] August Bebel (1840–1913), born in barracks at Cologne; son of a non-commissioned officer in the army; apprenticed for four years to a wood-turner; travelled as journeyman 1858-1860; tried to enter the army but rejected as unfit; went to Leipzig, where he found work, and threw himself into the development of the local Workmen's Improvement Society; became interested in politics as a Radical opposed to Lassalle; converted to Socialism partly by Liebknecht, and partly by reading Lassalle; elected to the North German Diet as a Democrat in 1867; set up for himself in business; elected to the Reichstag in 1871; prosecuted and imprisoned in 1871; was then employing a foreman, six journeymen and two apprentices; elected to the Reichstag while in prison; in 1874 took a partner in the business, which was the manufacture in a steam-driven factory of horn handles for doors and windows; in 1889 he retired from business, and on his death in 1913 left £50,000.

Liebknecht, expelled from Prussia, came to Leipzig. As an older and better educated man, the latter at once exercised considerable influence over Bebel, whom he instructed in the Marxian faith. Both were opposed to the Lassallean party and policy, and in 1869 founded a rival organisation called the 'Social Democratic Workmen's Party,' at a congress of the workmen's institutes, in which Bebel had for years been deeply interested. The rival organisations entered on an embittered conflict not only as political parties but also in regard to the formation of trade unions, which had been taken up a little earlier by Dr. Hirsch. Bebel assigns the birth of trade unionism in Germany to the year 1868, when Schweitzer for the Lassallean party entered into competition with Hirsch, and the Leipzig group started a movement against both under the influence of Liebknecht, who lectured on the English trade unions and aimed at creating unions in Germany in the service of Marxian Socialism.

There followed years of confused strife between and within the parties after the manner that has invariably marked all Socialist movements. The rival groups, as usual, were far more concerned to make their own ideas prevail than to achieve any practical result. Bebel himself is the witness:

> 'It cannot be denied that while the political movement was greatly impeded by dissensions the trade union movement suffered even more. None of the political groups would renounce the formation of its own special unions in the hope of securing increased power."[1]

[1] *Autobiography*, Cap. xi.

The fight for the trade unions has been carried on to this day, when several different kinds exist, but the political conflict was brought to an end by the fusion of the Lassalleans and Marxians in 1875, when a joint congress was held at Gotha and a common policy formulated. There was much discussion about the name to be given to the new organisation, and after several alternative proposals had been rejected the title 'Socialist Workmen's (or Labour) Party of Germany' (*Sozialistische Arbeiter Partei Deutschlands*) was adopted, but was later changed to 'Social-Democratic Party of Germany.' This title, which had come loosely into use during the period of Bismarck's anti-Socialist legislation (1878–1890) was formally adopted at the important Congress held at Erfurt in 1891, when the famous Erfurt programme was laid down. It differed widely from the previous Gotha programme, which had been a compromise between the Lassallean and Marxian doctrines. The new document revealed the triumph of the latter, of which it was and still is the authoritative and orthodox expression. Marx, who was in London all this time, had nothing directly to do with it, but he inspired it, chiefly through Liebknecht. Since it is one of the most important pronouncements in the history of Socialism it is desirable to quote at least the introduction, which laid down the theoretical basis of what has been the dominant form of Socialism ever since. It runs:

'The economic development of bourgeois society leads necessarily by its very nature to the disappearance of the small industry, the basis of which is the workman's ownership of his means of production. It separates the workman from those means and turns him into a propertyless proletarian, while the means of production become the monopoly of a relatively small number of capitalists and large land-owners.

'Hand in hand with this monopolisation of the means of production goes the supplanting of the scattered small concerns by colossal large ones, the evolution of the tool into the machine, and a gigantic increase in the productivity of human labour. But all the advantages of this transformation are monopolised by the capitalists and large land-owners. For the proletariat and the declining intermediate classes—small tradesmen and peasantry—it signified constantly increasing insecurity of existence, misery, oppression, servitude, debasement, exploitation.

'Ever greater grows the number of proletarians, ever vaster the army of superfluous workers, ever wider the gulf between the exploiters and exploited, ever more embittered the class-war between bourgeoisie and proletariat, which divides modern society into two hostile camps, and is the hall-mark of all industrial countries.

'The abyss between the owning and non-owning classes is further widened by the crises inherent in the capitalist method of production, which become ever more extensive and destructive, which raise general insecurity to the normal condition of society and furnish proof that modern productive forces have far outgrown society and that private ownership of the means of production has become quite incompatible with their proper application and full development.

'Private ownership of the means of production, which formerly secured to the producer the possession of his own product, has to-day become the means of expropriating peasants, handworkers, and small tradesmen and putting non-workers—capitalists and landowners—in possession of the product of the workers. Only the conversion of capitalist private ownership of the means of production—land and soil, mines and pits, raw materials, tools, machines, means of transport—into social ownership, and transformation of production for the market into Socialistic production carried on for and by society, can bring about the conversion of the large industry and the constantly increasing productivity of social labour from a source of misery and oppression for the hitherto exploited classes, into a source of the highest welfare and all-round harmonious perfection.

'This social transformation implies the emancipation not only of the proletariat but of the whole human race which is suffering under present conditions. But it can be accomplished only by the working class, because all other classes, in spite of conflicting interests among themselves, stand on the ground of private property in the means of production, and have as a common object preservation of the existing basis of society.

'The battle of the working class against capitalist exploitation is necessarily a political one. The working class cannot fight its economic battles or develop its economic organisation without political rights. It cannot achieve the transference of the means of production into the possession of the community without first securing possession of political power.

'To shape this battle of the working class into a conscious and united effort and to demonstrate its inevitable aim—this is the task of the Social-Democratic Party.

'The interests of the working class are identical in all countries where capitalist production prevails. With the expansion of world traffic and of production for the world market the condition of the workers in every country becomes ever more dependent on the condition of the workers in other countries. The emancipation of the working class is therefore a task in which the workers in all civilised countries are equally concerned. Recognising this, the Social-Democratic Party of Germany feels and declares itself one with the class-conscious workers of all other countries.

'The Social-Democratic Party of Germany is fighting, then, not for new class privileges or superior rights, but for the abolition of class rule and of classes themselves, for equal rights and equal duties for all without distinction of sex or birth. Setting out from this standpoint, it combats in existing society not merely the exploitation and oppression of the wage-earners, but every sort of exploitation and oppression, whether exercised against a class, a party, a sex or a race.'

The influence of Marx is written all over this pronouncement. The description of the economic conditions contained in the opening paragraphs merely recapitulates ideas already expressed in the Communist Manifesto forty-three years before and originally derived by Marx from Sismondi and the early French and English Socialists; but an exclusively Marxian touch is given by the emphasis laid on the inevitable character of the process, which it is assumed must go on progressively in the same direction, until it culminates, through the ever-worsening conditions created, in the predicted overthrow of the existing economic order and the transference of land and capital from private to public ownership.

This is the theory of increasing misery, and the assumption of inevitability is the distinguishing feature of 'Scientific Socialism,' which was invented by Marx and sharply contrasted, to his glorification, with all other forms of Socialism. The idea is embodied in the German word *naturnotwendig*, for which we have no equivalent in English. It means inevitable by nature, like a law of physical science, and it occurs twice in the Erfurt programme.

Now, as a matter of plain, historical fact, the process of social and economic development had not continued in the same direction, but had been greatly modified by 1891. What was true when Sismondi wrote and organised Socialism began in the first quarter of the 19th century no longer held good even in 1848, and much less in 1891. But the dogma had been laid down by Marx and must therefore be adhered to, though at variance with the facts. The discrepancy, however, was too glaring to be ignored and it led to a great division of opinion in the party on the subject of what is known as ' Revision.' The word is loosely used in two senses. It first came up at the annual congress in 1894, and from then onwards at intervals until 1905, when a grand debate took place on it. Bernstein, one of the leaders of the Party and a prominent revisionist, explained that the term referred to the theory, not the practice, of the party ; what needed revision was not the whole programme, but the first five paragraphs of the preamble and part of the sixth, because they did not correspond with the facts.

The chief trouble was the theory of increasing misery, to which the revisionists objected because misery was not increasing. This question was discussed at length in 1899, and two defences were offered : (1) that what was meant was only the tendency of misery to increase, (2) that what was meant was not absolute but relative misery. The word revision came to be applied, however, to the policy of the party in regard to social reform, and not only of the party but of Socialism in general. The connection is obvious. The theory of increasing misery leading to the complete overthrow of the existing order is inconsistent with the improvement of existing conditions by means of social reforms, which must postpone the grand consummation ; and the question arises—which path ought Socialists to pursue ? They cannot avoid the issue, because reforms are constantly being proposed and introduced by other parties. What should their attitude be ? The revisionists took the line of frankly promoting reforms, to which the other more revolutionary wing objected as playing the bourgeois game and sacrificing the specific principles of Socialism.

This difference has run through the whole movement and always divided it into a right and left wing, not only in Germany, but everywhere. In Germany the party held together as a political unit in spite of heated disputes, mainly through the German sense of discipline and the skilful leadership of Bebel, who was always more of a politician than a theoretical Socialist; but elsewhere the division took more open effect and became a great source of weakness, particularly in France. On the surface the difference appears to be merely a matter of the relative stress laid on the final revolutionary aim and on the immediate practical questions of the day; but it really goes much deeper. It reflects the clash between fact and theory, between things as they are and as Marx pictured them. This contradiction is fundamental and fatal to the theory, to which orthodox Marxians nevertheless cling because it chimes with their wishes and they can think of nothing to replace it. The lack of original ideas characterising the whole second phase of Socialism is very clearly illustrated by this sterile repetition of old formulas. Many Marxians, conscious of the discrepancy between reality and hypothesis, have said that if Marx had lived he would have modified his views, and he probably would. Both he and Engels did change their views very considerably during their lives, and twenty years before the Erfurt programme admitted, in a new edition of the Communist Manifesto, that it had become antiquated in some respects; but neither was an original thinker, and it is doubtful if they were capable of any new and vital ideas that would really answer to the march of events.

At any rate, their followers were not. They met the difficulty by combining discordant propositions. They repeated the old phrases of the Communist Manifesto about the proletariat and the bourgeoisie, elimination of the small concerns by the large (concentration of capital), increasing misery, etc., leading inevitably to the economic revolution to be accomplished by the roused proletariat, not by force, however, as in the Communist Manifesto, but by political action ; and having thus paid formal homage to the dogma, they proceeded to tack on to it a programme of reforms, electoral, financial and social, tending to a more democratic constitution and improvement of the condition of the proletariat, but differing from any Radical programme only by being more comprehensive and going rather farther in some respects. The principal items were the following :

Universal adult (twenty years) suffrage ; proportional representation ; initiative and referendum ; universal military service for national militia ; decisions on war and peace by representatives of the people ; free speech and free meetings ; legal and social equality of sexes ; religion to be a private matter, no public funds to be devoted to clerical or religious purposes ; secular public education ; gratuitous administration of justice and advocacy ; elected judges, the right of appeal from sentences, abolition of the death penalty ; gratuitous medical treatment and burial ; graduated income tax and death duties ; abolition of indirect taxation. Also labour legislation (national and international), including an eight hours' day, abolition of child labour under fourteen and of night-work except on technical grounds, weekly rest of at least thirty-six hours, abolition of truck, supervision and inspection of working conditions, thorough industrial hygiene, agricultural and domestic workers to have the same legal rights as industrial workers, the right of combination, the whole system of workmen's insurance to be taken over by the State and administered with joint control by the workmen.

Not a single item in the programme has anything to do with the 'conversion of capitalist private ownership of the means of production into social ownership,' declared in the preamble to be the sole means of attaining the great end and abolishing the evils described. Facts were too strong for theory. When it came to practical politics, Socialism was relegated to a pious expression of opinion, and the actual measures officially adopted by the party were reforms intended to modify the existing system but not to change its essential character.

And that was the part played all through by the German Socialists. They assisted in shaping reforms, and used their growing strength to that end; they have all been revisionists in fact, whatever they might say. They could in truth do nothing else for two reasons—first because the proletariat, who are their clients, did not wish to sink deeper and deeper into misery in order to promote a glorious change in some indefinite future, but on the contrary demanded immediate relief; and secondly, because the alternative was to condemn themselves to complete sterility. At the last Congress of the party held before the war in 1913, some dissatisfaction was expressed, and the Reichstag members, in giving an account of their stewardship, took an apologetic tone; but the Congress endorsed their revisionist tactics by 333 to 142 votes, and Dr. Frank, of Mannheim, one of the ablest members, declared that the old uncompromising attitude was obsolete. He argued that reform tactics were really in accordance with their principles, because though they apparently bolstered up the capitalist system they actually strengthened the working classes. The argument is ingenious and has force, but it throws over scientific Socialism.

The progress of the party in Parliamentary strength is shown in the following table, which gives the results of successive general elections after the formation of the Empire.

REICHSTAG ELECTIONS

Year	Votes cast for Socialists	Percentage of total votes	Socialists elected
1871	124,655	3.2	2
1874	351,952	6.8	10
1877	493,288	9.1	13
1878	437,158	7.6	9
1881	311,961	6.1	13
1884	549,990	9.7	24

REICHSTAG ELECTIONS—(*continued*)

Year	Votes cast for Socialists	Percentage of total votes	Socialists elected
1887	763,128	10.1	11
1890	1,427,298	19.7	35
1893	1,786,738	23.3	44
1898	2,107,076	27.2	56
1903	3,010,771	31.7	81
1907	3,259,020	28.9	43
1912	4,250,329	34.8	110

During the forty-one years the party had grown from insignificance to be the largest group in the Reichstag, and the percentage of votes cast for it had increased more than tenfold. The percentage is a better index than the number of votes cast because the electorate was steadily increasing all the time and nearly doubled between 1871 and 1912. The percentage is also a better index of electoral strength than the number elected, because that is subject to the caprice of luck. The great drop in members from 1903 to 1907 and the subsequent still greater rise in 1912 were both largely due to luck.

But perhaps the most interesting feature of the table is the movement of the party during the bracketed period 1878–1890, covering the duration of Bismarck's anti-Socialist laws. This repressive legislation, which followed an attempt to shoot Kaiser Wilhelm I. out driving in Berlin, was enacted after the 1878 election, and was renewed at intervals until the beginning of 1890, when it fell through in consequence of party strife between Liberals and Conservatives. Its effect is shown by the drop of votes in 1881 and its failure by the subsequent rise in 1884 and 1887. Its expiry in 1890 found the Socialist Party about thrice as strong as it had been before the law was passed. The several parties in the Reichstag, exclusive of some small, special and indefinite groups, and their strength at three successive stages are shown in the following table:

REICHSTAG PARTIES

Party	1871	1890	1912
Conservative	57	73	42
Imperial (Reichs-Partei)	37	20	14
National Liberal	125	42	45
Progressive (Fortschritt)	46	—	—
Radical (Freisininige)	—	66	—
Popular (Volkspartei)	—	—	42
Centre	63	106	93
Polish	13	16	18
Alsatian	—	10	7
Social-Democratic	2	35	110

From the smallest the Socialists had become the largest group, mainly at the expense of Liberals and Radicals. Out of 397 total members they counted 110, or very nearly 28 per cent. But their progress was still greater electorally; they polled more than one-third of the votes cast, and if the representation had been in strict numerical proportion they would have had 138 members. Their strength lay naturally in the large urban centres and industrial districts, which had undergone a rapid increase in population, without a redistribution of seats.

It must not be inferred, however, that because 4½ million electors voted for Socialist candidates in 1912 there were so many Socialists in Germany then. The voters must not be confused with the Party itself, which is an organisation of professed Socialists, who prove their faith by the convincing test of paying subscriptions. In 1875, when the two previous groups came together, as described above, and formed the party proper, they had fewer than 25,000 members. The income for the first year was £2,700, out of which eight whole-time propagandists were maintained at a salary of £80 a year, besides a number of other paid officers. One of the secrets of the success of Socialism in Germany is the use made of the Press, particularly in the form of daily and weekly newspapers. Almost from the first the movement had its own papers, to which the most distinguished leaders contributed, and they continually increased in number. By 1876 there were 23 and in 1877 43 political and 14 labour papers. In 1913 the number of journals had increased to 92. No details of the membership are available after 1875 until 1906, but the annual income rose from £2,700 to £11,200 in 1891 and to £59,590 in 1908. The membership from 1906 down to the War is given in the following table :

MEMBERSHIP OF SOCIAL-DEMOCRATIC PARTY

Year	Total Members	Female Members.
1906	384,327	—
1907	530,466	10,943
1908	587,336	29,458
1909	633,309	62,259
1910	720,038	82,642
1911	836,562	107,693
1912	970,112	130,371
1913	982,850	141,115

An examination of the last two years reveals two curious facts : (1) that the rate of increase had fallen enormously, and (2) that almost the whole of what there was occurred in the women's side. The male membership, which had increased by 120,000 in 1911–12, had become stationary.

The numerical strength of the party was derived mainly from the trade unions, the beginnings of which have already been described. They originated in spontaneous trade combinations of workmen as far back as 1843, when the printers formed one. Both the Lassallean and the Marxian Socialist parties were against the trade unions until Dr. Hirsch, a Radical, took up the organisation of labour on the English model, whereupon the Socialist Parties began to cultivate them in rivalry, all for political ends. Eventually there came to be five or six kinds of organisation, but of these only four, or perhaps three, were trade unions in our sense of the word. These were: (1) the Free or Social-Democratic, (2) the Christian, and (3) the German or Hirsch-Duncker unions. The third and smallest group was the only one with a continuous history from 1869; the first and much the largest group was submerged under the anti-Socialist laws and re-appeared in 1891; the second was founded later, in 1900. It was the first group that supported the Socialist Party, though without any formal connection, and their rapid growth—from 277,659 in 1891 to 2,553,162 in 1912—coincided with the progress of the party in the constituencies. The much smaller Christian and 'German' unions were hostile.

But since the votes cast for the party in 1912 exceeded the total membership of the 'free' unions by 1¾ millions it is obvious that a large measure of support was drawn from other sources. The Socialist Party was, in fact, a refuge for voters of all kinds who were dissatisfied with other parties, or with things in general. The Socialist vote, then, represented three grades of support: (1) the inner ring of Socialists, (2) an outer and larger ring of non-Socialist trade-unionists, (3) an outside ring of discontented persons. The position since the War is dealt with in Part II.

Chapter IV

THE SECOND PHASE (*continued*)

France and Great Britain

In France the second phase of Socialism began several years later than in Germany. No definite movement can be discerned before 1879, when Marxian Socialism emerged victorious, for the time being, from the clash of ideas in which it struggled with the surviving relics of the old Socialism and with a spontaneous trade union movement that had arisen after the war with Germany in 1870.

After the Revolution of 1848, in which Socialism was forcibly suppressed, public attention was mainly absorbed first in politics and the re-establishment of the Empire, which was consummated in 1853, and later by a series of wars—with Russia (the Crimean war) in 1854–55, with Austria in 1859–60, with Mexico in 1861–65, and finally with Germany in 1870–71, followed by the Commune and the re-establishment of the Republic. During this period, also, a vast expansion of industry and commerce took place and produced a corresponding state of prosperity. Amid these distractions and occupations Socialism, though not extinct or altogether silent, made little impression and no advance.

The most influential voice was that of Proudhon, who in 1863 published his *Capacity of the Working*

Classes, which caught their ear. In it he recognised the class-war, but urged a peaceful solution. He protested against the cure of one class-oppression by another and maintained that the object of the working-class should be not to abolish the just rights of the middle classes, but to acquire for themselves the same liberty of action and so fuse the social classes. Mutualism, reciprocity of services and co-operation were the salient features of his teaching, and of course it clashed violently with Marxism, which at this time began to be pushed outside Germany, as well as inside by the First International (see Chapter VI). It is impossible to say what might have become of these tendencies because they were all submerged in the Franco-German war.

The catastrophe led to the Commune of March, 1871, which presented an amorphous welter of different and really antagonistic elements flung together by popular excitement. It included traditions of the Great Revolution—notably attacks on the Church and religion—mixed up with divergent strains of Socialism, both Proudhonian and Marxian. There was much talk about the proletariat, and one proclamation announced the 'progressive universalisation of property,' whatever that might mean. Real workmen took an active part and proclaimed ideal aims; the re-establishment of the national workshops was demanded among other things, and traces of international Socialism revealed themselves. But as a whole the rising was rather political than economic so far as it had any definite character at all beyond an exhibition of violence. The predominant influence was that of

Blanqui, the veteran revolutionary conspirator, and the effect of the outbreak was purely destructive. Unsupported by the Provinces, which were in general opposed to it, the Paris rising was suppressed in May; but in the following September, when passing through on my way back to school in England, I saw the burnt-out public buildings and the remains of barricades still in the streets.

The first movement that followed came from the trade unions which had been encouraged under the Empire by the removal of some legal disabilities, and it had nothing of Socialism in it. Begun in 1872, this trade union movement, though severely harried again under the new Republic, had advanced sufficiently to hold a congress of some importance in 1876. It was the first Labour Congress in France, and its aims were definitely pacific and co-operative. But in the same year Jules Guesde, the consistent champion of Marxism returned from exile and at once set to work to capture the Congress. A struggle ensued in which the co-operators held their own at successive congresses until 1879, when intellectuals as well as trade unionists were admitted and the principles of the class-war and socialisation of land and capital were adopted by 73 to 27 votes.

This congress, held at Marseilles, marked the foundation of the Socialist-Labour Party in France, under the title of 'Federation of the Party of Socialist Workers of France.' Its formation was to be consummated at the following congress to be held at Havre in 1880, for which purpose Guesde repaired to London to draw up a programme with Marx and Engels; but he was not to have it all his own way. His programme, which followed the usual Marxian lines and advocated collectivism, was approved in Paris, but met with a stout resistance from the trade unionists in the large provincial towns which are traditionally and instinctively opposed to the influence of Paris. The men of Havre in particular were determined that the meeting should be a real labour congress, not one of 'bourgeois theorists,' and laid down the reasonable condition that only delegates representing a group of at least twenty-five members should be admitted. This split the new party in two. Guesde, who was as intolerant of opposition as Marx himself, withdrew to another hall and held a separate congress with his followers.

The conflict, thus begun by Socialism within the Labour movement, was destined to last for twenty-five years in various forms. It is a tedious and tangled story not worth telling in detail; and by the time it was nominally ended in 1905 another and a far more significant line of cleavage had established itself. This was Syndicalism, which emerged in full force in 1902. A brief review of the intervening period must suffice. The principal fact was the growth of trade unionism after 1884, when the legal disabilities, which had repressed the movement ever since the great Revolution, were removed by abrogation of the law of 1791 prohibiting all combinations. The sixty-eight trade unions existing in 1884 had become more than 1,000 in 1890 and 2,685 in 1900; and where the carcase was, there the eagles or vultures were gathered together. The Socialist groups, multiplying by division, fought for control of the unions.

The first split in 1880, related above, was soon followed by a second in 1882, when Guesde and his followers quarrelled with Brousse and left the organisation they had founded themselves. Another split followed before long between Brousse and Allemane, and in 1890 there were four Socialist parties in the field: (1) French Labour Party (Guesdist and Marxian), (2) Federation of Socialist Workers (Broussist and Reformist), (3) Socialist Revolutionary Labour Party (Allemanist), (4) Socialist Revolutionary Party (Blanquist and largely Anarchist). Later a fifth group of Independents was formed. The first of these groups had most success with the growing trade unions, who held a national congress in 1886, at which it was decided to form a national federation. In the following year the Guesdist principles were adopted, but with the general strike added on to them.

In that same year, however, a little cloud appeared upon the horizon. The first *bourse du travail* was opened in Paris. The word means literally 'labour exchange,' and that was the original idea; but the thing itself came to correspond much more closely to our 'trades council,' that is a local organisation embracing all the unions in the district. Other towns soon set up *bourses* of their own, and there were thus two forms of trade union organisation. In 1892 the *bourses* formed a federation of their own and the two federations became rivals, once more illustrating the extraordinary tendency of the French to disagree. Now since the Guesdists had more or less captured the Federation of Unions, the other Socialists naturally looked to the federation of *bourses* for support; and they found a favourable soil for cultivating at least opposition to Marxian political Socialism and the prospect of State Collectivism.

But gradually a purely labour policy was evolved, very much as in England in 1833. To make the resemblance complete, the idea of the general strike, first put forward in England in 1831,[1] reappeared in exactly the same form. The syndicalist policy grew up round this idea, which greatly appealed to French workmen. It was a flag, a slogan calling to action and perfectly suited to their psychology; even the Guesdist unions rallied to it. The heavy Marxian economics had bored them to death; Guesde's intolerable arrogance repelled them, and the sterility of his Parliamentary policy disillusioned them. They were ready for something new, more tangible, and their own. It was this idea that brought the two federations together.

In 1894 a joint congress was held at which the general strike was adopted after a set debate, and the following year saw the formation of the General Confederation of Labour and the inauguration of 'Syndicalism,' in the technical sense of a militant labour movement independent of all politics and especially opposed to State Socialism. The fusion of the two wings was completed in 1902 and the new movement established on a firm basis. Its aim was capture of the means of production by the workmen engaged in each industry, and abolition of the State; the means were the general strike and *sabotage*, which is any action that damages

[1] See p. 29.

the interest of the present owners or employers, whether private persons or public bodies, who were equally regarded as enemies. This policy is obviously more anarchist than socialist in that it would abolish the State, but it differs from anarchism proper in that it would not establish that complete individual freedom which is the supreme object of anarchism. The trade unions would be free and autonomous, but the individual workmen would be controlled by the organisation. The expression 'direct action,' which has since become famous in England, was coined by the French Syndicalists. They did not formulate any clearly constructive policy; and the organisation, though nominally united, was soon weakened by division into right and left wings, and by the standing resistance offered by large provincial towns to the domination of Paris.

The principle of Syndicalism was the most original idea that emerged in the second phase of Socialism, and even that was a revival—a spontaneous and unconscious revival—of the English movement of 1831–34.[1] But the motive was different. French Syndicalists argued that the State was too oppressive already and if it controlled industry life would be intolerable. The new movement naturally attracted much attention and attempts were made to transplant it to other countries, but with little visible success except where anarchist tendencies were strong, as in the Latin countries. Nevertheless, it has exercised a powerful and general influence, and has everywhere modified the Socialist conception of the

[1] See p. 29.

new order by bringing in the idea of the control of industry by those engaged in it. In France the General Confederation, which numbered about half a million members before the war, actually achieved nothing but a large number of (generally abortive) strikes; but it affected the political situation, and was a source of weakness to the Socialist Parties, to which I now return.

They made no mark in the Chamber of Deputies until 1893. Their first electoral campaign in 1885 produced only 60,000 votes; in 1889, seven members were returned; in 1893, there were 43. They then entered on a period of considerable Parliamentary activity and acquired a new standing in the public eye, due not only to their number, but also to the personality of certain members, particularly Jean Jaurès, who forsook the Radicals and took up Socialism in 1892. A professor of philosophy, a man of the highest culture and a most accomplished orator, he commanded general respect and esteem, and from 1893 Socialism became 'respectable.' M. Millerand was another member who commanded respect by his ability and knowledge of social questions. In 1896, he gave a famous address on Socialism to representatives of the Socialist parties, and defined a conception of Socialism which was unanimously accepted. It is virtually identical with that of our own Labour Party to-day—gradual and progressive socialisation of the means of production by constitutional methods.

Both he and Jaurès were working then for unity, which was eventually achieved by Jaurès in 1905, when the 'French Socialist Party' (Reformist) and the 'Socialist Party of France' (Revolutionary), joined hands, but in the interval, M. Millerand had created a great stir and revived antagonisms by entering the 'bourgeois' Waldeck-Rosseau Ministry in 1899. This incident revealed the gulf between orthodox Marxian Socialism and Reformism, and sent a shock throughout the Socialist world. The electoral address of the Unified Party in 1906 was a summarised paraphrase of the Erfurt programme —class war, increasing misery, conquest of political power, socialisation of the means of production, etc. The political progress of the party is shown in the following table of general elections:

Year	Votes Received	Members Elected
1902	805,000	48
1906	877,999	54
1910	1,106,047	76

The Parliamentary strength of the Party in a Chamber of 577, and still more its voting strength in the constituencies, were small compared with the corresponding position of the Party in Germany, and its actual membership comparatively trifling, being less than 70,000. But these figures do not reflect the real position in France. The Unified Party, though nominally embracing the old groups, did not include all the Socialist elements; there were, in addition, 34 Independent Socialist Deputies in the Chamber, and 150 Radical Socialists, meaning Radicals leaning towards Socialism, but not of it. The French had not moved towards Socialism in the solid manner of the Germans, but they had moved more than appeared on the surface. The net result was to promote a policy of reform in which the moderate wing of the Socialist Party—still divided by internal differences though 'unified'—could join, while the left wing was condemned to sterility.

In short, the practical upshot was much the same as in Germany, though the party grouping was different. As Socialism increased its strength it might retain its policy, but being confronted with sterility or reform had to adjust its action to circumstances. The example of M. Millerand in joining a bourgeois Ministry was followed by other prominent leaders, by M. Viviani and M. Briand, who had assisted Jaurès in founding the important newspaper, *L'Humanité*, in 1904. Before this paper appeared French Socialism had been very weak in literature and particularly in periodicals, in contrast with Germany and its own early phase. Its increasing strength just before the war was shown at the general election of 1914, when the Socialists polled 1,391,373 votes and had 102 deputies returned. The membership of the party had then risen to 93,000.

Some mention must be made of its municipal activity, which began earlier and advanced much more rapidly than its parliamentary efforts. Dating from 1882, when Socialist councillors were returned in some provincial towns, it speedily gained complete control in so many provincial towns that in ten years' time a congress of Socialist municipalities was organised. This success brought theory to the test of practice, with the result that the administration of affairs on Socialist principles led to such a state of financial disorder as to cause its abandonment by general consent in one town after another. Outside the town the peasantry—small working landowners—have always been opposed to Socialism, and since they are very numerous in France, their resistance formed an obstacle which compelled a revision of principles and the toleration of small capitalists. So matters stood before the war, when on its very eve, French Socialism sustained a great loss by the assassination of Jaurès. On November 23, 1924, his remains were removed from the cemetery where they had lain and deposited in the Pantheon with great ceremony at the national expense.

Great Britain

The revival of Socialism came considerably later in Great Britain, although London was the birthplace of the first International in 1864. This organisation, which is described in Chapter VII, was directed by Marx, and the fact that it rather repelled than attracted the trade unions, which it was intended to capture, shows how little the doctrine associated with it appealed to the new generation. The former movement had left no live shoots behind, as in France, and was indeed generally forgotten. Even surviving leaders had changed their minds. William Lovett, who has been justly called the 'hero' of Chartism, left a striking recantation of principle, in his autobiography. Writing of the theory of collective ownership and common use of modern powers of production, he says it was most attractive to 'the plodding, toiling, ill-remunerated sons and daughters of labour' and most captivating to 'those who accept the idea without investigation.'

'I was one,' he continues, 'who accepted this grand idea of machinery working for the benefit of all, without considering that those powers and inventions have been chiefly called forth and industriously and efficiently applied by the stimulus *our industrial system has afforded*, and that the benefits to the originators and successful workers of them—though large in some instances—have been few and trifling compared to the benefits *which millions now enjoy* from their general application. Those great results, too, have hitherto been realised by the hope of wealth, fame or station, *keeping up man's energies to the tension point*. But who can foresee what human beings may become when the *individualism* in their nature is checked by education and endeavoured to be crushed out of them by the mandate of a majority—and it may be that majority not always a reasonable and enlightened one? Of what advantage the splendour and enjoyment of all art and nature *if man has no choice of enjoyment?* And what to him would be spacious halls and luxurious apartments and all the promised blessings of a community, if he must rise, work, dress, occupy and enjoy, not as he himself desires, *but as the fiat of the majority wills it?* Surely the poorest labourer, bowed down with toil and poverty, would have reason to bless the individualism that gave him some freedom of choice and a chance of improving his lot, compared with a fellowship that so bound him in bondage. But we shall be told of the perfect and wise arrangements that are so to perfect human character that no man "shall ever need to be b amed for his conduct," nor men ever have occasion to make their fellows "responsible for their actions." Unfortunately the great obstacle to the realisation of this perfect state of things is that the perfect and wise arrangements are to depend on *imperfect men and women.*"

Elsewhere he says:

'When so much remains to be done for the upraising of our people, you should not waste your energies on vain theories, impractical measures, nor in empty threats or denunciations. All such doings, therefore, and all talk about the condemnation of capital which is the heart's blood of an industrial nation—all denunciation of property, or foolish threats of confiscation, tend to social discord and alarm; and to cause all who possess property to place it if possible beyond the reach of danger and to flee to despots for protection, as the least of evils; and it should also be remembered that, in all civil commotions, it is the poor and innocent that first suffer. Large accumulations of capital and a vast amount of wealth, have doubtless, in many instances, been acquired by injustice; but in seeking a remedy we should be wise as well as just, for the stability of our whole social fabric would be greatly endangered by any attempts to interfere with *the just rights of property.* The true remedy

[1] *Life and Struggles of William Lovett*, 1920, Vol. I, p. 45–6.

will lie in such peaceful and efficient reforms as shall prevent such unjust accumulations in future, and to prevent such masses of wealth from being made instruments of oppression and injustice.'[1]

These reflections by a workman, who not only witnessed but experienced the conditions that brought Socialism into being as an organised movement—he came to London in 1821—and who played a prominent part in developing the movement, help to explain the long eclipse and slow revival of Socialism in this country. An entirely new generation had arisen when the revival came, which was not until the decade 1880–90. Even then the earliest organisation to be formed was not at first socialist but merely representative of advanced radicalism.

This was the Social Democratic Federation, founded in 1881 without the word Social, which was not introduced until 1884, when a programme of political reforms was adopted, but containing also the nationalisation of land,[2] and when a weekly newspaper was started, to propagate the policy. The paper was *Justice*, which has kept the flag flying through all vicissitudes until now. The leaders were intellectuals, and the German inspiration was revealed in the title, but their ideas were vague, dissensions arose, and before three months had passed the inevitable split occurred. William Morris, with other prominent members, seceded to form a more revolutionary group called the Socialist

[1] *Life and Struggles of William Lovett*, 1920, Vol. II, p. 434–5.

[2] This is according to *Justice* No. 1; the account given by Mr. Beer is somewhat different.

League, leaving the late Henry Hyndman to lead the parent organisation, which he had founded.

It gradually became more definitely Marxian under his influence, and adopted a programme which declared that labour is the source of all wealth, and therefore all wealth belongs to labour, that the production of wealth should be regulated by society in the common interest of all, and that the means of production should be collective property—all the old formulas. The class war was not at first mentioned, but it was implicit in the principles of the society, and later energetically preached. The S.D.F. furnished the first Socialist candidates for Parliament in 1885, when three of its members stood, but met with a chilly response. The most successful was John Burns, who polled 598 votes; the others failed to reach three figures. Nor did the society ever succeed in having one of its members elected as such until Mr. Dan Irving was returned for Burnley in 1918, after many previous failures. On the other hand it had, before the war, about 150 representatives on local public bodies, including 40 town councillors. The total membership was then believed to be about 10,000. The society has never exercised much direct influence, but as a school of Socialism it has played a considerable part in educating propagandists. It has had a chequered career, having undergone various divisions and changes of name and programme, which need not be recorded, but it has always maintained a sturdy independence. In 1911 it became the British Socialist Party. The dissentient Socialist League became anarchist, and had a very short career.

Next in chronological order is the Fabian Society, founded in 1884. Since the older society just described took a definitely socialistic form at the same time, that year may be regarded as dating the re-birth of Socialism, sixty years after the first phase and twenty years later than the beginning of the second phase in Germany. The influence of the Fabian Society during the forty years of its existence has been too subtle to be measured, but it has certainly been very great. It has been wholly intellectual, and exercised through many channels by a policy of permeation, though individual members have also taken part in public life; the most prominent instance is the work of Mr. Sidney Webb on the London County Council. He and Mr. Bernard Shaw are the best known Fabians, but the society has been a school for young intellectuals all along, and their multiplication in recent years, especially at the universities, is probably due to it more than to any other agency. Influence of this kind does not depend on numbers, which appear never to have reached 3,000.

The principles of the Society are essentially collectivist, it 'aims at the re-organisation of society by the emancipation of land and industrial capital from individual and class ownership and the vesting of them in the community for the general benefit,' but insists on constitutional means, and puts forward a moderate programme of reforms. It is the least Marxian and the least combative of the British organisations, and though devoid of original ideas is distinguished by the stress it lays on local government and municipal activity. It has worked in close connection with the next body to be mentioned, the Independent Labour Party, which may be regarded as an agency for translating Fabian ideas into political action.

The Independent Labour Party, not to be confounded with the Labour Party, is a Socialist society, like the preceding. It was founded at Bradford in 1893, at a conference of delegates from pre-existing Socialist bodies under the chairmanship of Keir Hardie, a Scottish miner, who had been elected to Parliament with John Burns in 1892. Different accounts of its origin are given in Socialist publications. Keir Hardie's own account is that about 1890, when there was much ferment in the trade union world, Socialist organisations began to spring up spontaneously in different places, and that these came together at Bradford. The earliest was the Scottish Labour Party formed in 1889. Another account is that in 1892 some members of the Social Democratic Federation, feeling that their society was too academic and uncompromising to make much progress towards the goal, resolved to form another organisation better calculated to secure the sympathies and co-operation of organised labour, and the conference was the result.

The two accounts are quite compatible. The I.L.P. was, in fact, formed in order to bring together the streams of Socialism and organised labour like the movement of 1831. At the inaugural meeting its object was stated to be 'to secure the collective and communal ownership of all the means of production, distribution and exchange.' Later, verbal changes were introduced without altering the sense. At one time the object was to establish 'an industrial commonwealth founded upon the socialisation of land and capital.' In 1906, the new order was to be

> 'the Socialist State, when land and capital will be held by the community and used for the well-being of the community, and when the exchange of commodities will be organised, also by the community, so as to secure the highest possible standard of life for the individual.'

The latest formula declares for the 'Socialist Commonwealth,' which is

> 'that State of Society in which land and Capital are communally owned and the processes of production, distribution and exchange are social functions.'

As with the other organisations, the statement of its object was followed by a programme of social and political reforms, which has also undergone various modifications.

From the first the I.L.P. grew quickly and made some progress in the task of enlisting organised labour under the banner of Socialism, though the leaders still shrank from adopting the term officially in the title of the society. Their aim was to detach the trade unions from the Liberal Party, and 'Independent Labour Party'—a title first used by the Scottish Labour Party just mentioned—was thought more attractive. But they overrated their electoral influence, and at the general election of 1895 put up twenty-eight candidates, without any success; Keir Hardie himself lost his seat. Ten years were to elapse before success came. The record before the war was as follows:

Year	Candidates	Votes received	Elected
1895	28	44,594	0
1900	10	37,207	1
1905	10	76,494	8
1910 (Jan.)	15	92,081	6
1910 (Dec.)	12	69,884	8

The table refers only to candidates standing as direct representatives of the I.L.P., and does not include members of the society standing under other auspices. In 1910 there were 15 such members elected as representing trade unions, in addition to the eight official I.L.P. representatives. The society had then a membership of approximately 30,000, and over 1,000 representatives on local public bodies. It was by far the largest of the Socialist organisations in the country, and very active in propaganda of every kind by the written and spoken word. A weekly paper, the *Labour Leader*, evolved in 1893 by Keir Hardie out of a small sheet for Scottish miners, was gradually supplemented by some dozen local weeklies. The Society also produced a monthly, the *Socialist Review*, many booklets and innumerable pamphlets and leaflets.

The three societies described were the chief organisations concerned in the revival of Socialism in Great Britain; but there were some others which must be briefly mentioned to make the story complete. In 1891 Mr. Robert Blatchford, who was not an intellectual, but an ex-soldier, started a weekly Socialist paper called the *Clarion.* The master of an admirably simple but vigorous and expressive style, through which shone an engaging personality, he made a far more popular appeal than any other Socialist writer, and gradually gathered about the paper a loose but extensive organisation of Clarion clubs and Clarion scouts. His books, *Merrie England* and *Britain for the British,* had a great vogue, and it is doubtful if any individual anywhere has ever done so much to popularise Socialism ; but he was no Marxian. On the contrary, he breathed the spirit of the earlier phase of Socialism—the spirit of good-will and sympathy with the 'bottom dog.'

No country has been so resistent to Marxism as Great Britain, though Marx and Engels lived here, and the International was born in London. Even the Social Democratic Federation were not thorough-going disciples, but assumed an independent attitude and advocated reformism. This eventually led to a repetition of the split of 1884 mentioned above. The more revolutionary elements once more seceded and formed two new bodies, the Socialist Labour Party in Scotland (1903) and the Socialist Party of Great Britain in London (1905). These extreme exponents of revolutionary Marxism supplied the nucleus of the post-war Communist Party. In 1911 the Clarion organisations were absorbed, with some other elements, by the Social Democratic Party (formerly Federation), which again changed its name to British Socialist Party.

It will be seen from this account that the Socialist

organisations which arose in the second phase in this country were as numerous as in France and equally divided, from the Fabians on the extreme right to the Socialist Labour Party on the extreme left, with the rest in between and leaning towards one side or the other; but the balance of strength lay decisively with the right wing, which combined intellectual superiority (the Fabian) with numerical superiority (the I.L.P.), and through the latter influenced the trade unions. This distribution of strength is a fact of the greatest importance, because it determined the character and policy of the Labour Party, to which we now come.

The Labour Party was originally formed in 1900, and it may be regarded in one sense as an expression of the failure of the Independent Labour Party to capture the working class electorate. The Trades Union Congress had set up a Parliamentary Committee in 1869, and there had for many years been direct representatives of trade unions in Parliament. The first to be elected were Alexander MacDonald for Stafford and Thomas Burt for Norfolk in 1874, both representing miners; in 1880 they were joined by Henry Broadhurst, representing the building trades, and in 1885 by several more. But this Labour representation was quite different from the later movement. The early Labour members were politically Liberals; they were returned to Parliament, not to form a separate party, but merely to represent special interests and contribute special knowledge within the standing party arrangement. A movement in that direction had been in progress for some years before 1874, and the two Labour members then elected were merely the successful candidates out of a total of thirteen.

There was nothing of Socialism about them; its appearance on the scene came later, as related above, and its Parliamentary ventures were at first unsuccessful, though the number of trade union M.P's. continued to increase. Nor did the Labour Party itself assume a Socialist complexion at first. It began as the Labour Representation Committee, which was formed early in 1900 at a joint meeting of delegates from trade unions and socialist societies, in accordance with a resolution passed at the Trades Union Congress of 1899, but drafted by the I.L.P. Mr. Ramsay MacDonald was made secretary of the new body, which consisted of representatives of trade unions, the I.L.P., the Fabian Society, and Social Democratic Party, but the last named withdrew in the following year. The co-operative societies refused the invitation to join. The total membership of the bodies represented by the L.R.C. on its formation was 375,931, of whom 22,861 were Socialists and the rest trade unionists. They put up 15 candidates at the general election in 1900 and had two elected, namely Keir Hardie and Richard Bell, then secretary of the railwaymen's union and not a Socialist. Two or three more were added at subsequent bye-elections, but it was in 1906 that the L.R.C. made its great advance and took the name, Labour Party. At the general election that year it put up 50 candidates, of whom 29 were returned. At the same election the miners' unions, which were not affiliated, returned 16 members of their own, and other trade unions also sent representatives to

Parliament, bringing the total number of members who claimed or were popularly given the title 'Labour Members' up to 54.

The main reason for this remarkable change in the Parliamentary situation was the Taff Vale judgment, a legal decision obtained in 1901 by the Taff Vale Railway Company against the Amalgamated Society of Railway Servants (now the National Union of Railwaymen). The final ruling of the law courts was that under the existing law a registered trade union could be sued and held responsible for any damage inflicted by illegal acts on the part of its servants, agents, or members acting on its authority. The Taff Vale Railway Company took advantage of this decision to extract a large sum from the union for damages caused by a strike, and the South Wales coal-owners took similar action against the miners' union.

The judgment was hailed by short-sighted persons as a great triumph for employers as against trade unions; they forgot that the law could be altered, and the whole trade union world was resolved to alter it. There never was a more disastrous triumph for the victors. The result was the election of 1906 and the passing of the Trade Disputes Act, which employers and others have never ceased to bewail; they owe it to their South Wales colleagues. No other employers made use of the judgment; and it is no mere coincidence that since that date South Wales, which was once the most peaceful area in the country, has become the most disturbed, and a great centre of revolutionary agitation. Thus do certain employers provide their enemies with ammunition and lay up trouble for everybody, but particularly for themselves.

The progress of the Labour Party before the war is shown in the following table:

Year	Membership of affiliated bodies	Candidates	Votes received	Elected
1900	375,931	15	62,698	2
1906	921,280	50	323,196	29
1910 (Jan.)	1,430,539	78	505,690	40
1910 (Dec.)	1,430,539	56	370,802	42

With regard to the second column, the great increase in numbers is due entirely to the trade unions affiliating to the party. In the ten years, 1900–1910, the membership of the Socialist societies adhering increased only from 22,861 to 31,377, while the number of unions rose from 41 to 151 and their membership from 353,070 to 1,394,402, chiefly through the adhesion of the miners in 1908. In this connection, it should be remembered that the total strength of an affiliated union is given as supporting the Party, though affiliation is decided by a bare majority, so that dissentients and indifferents, who may together outnumber the others, are all reckoned in as supporters of the party. And not only that, they also had to contribute through the union to the financial support of the party. That is to say, the principle of majority rule, which was accepted for the ordinary purposes of trade unions, was extended to political purposes, and union money equally contributed by all members was used to promote a policy of which some, and in many cases a large number, strongly disapproved; Liberal and Conservative trade unionists were paying against their will for anti-Liberal and anti-Conservative candidates.

At first this new development did not give rise to trouble, because the declared object, formally adopted in 1901, was merely to form a 'distinct labour group in Parliament,' ready to 'co-operate with any party engaged in promoting legislation in the direct interest of labour,' or in 'opposing measures having an opposite tendency.' The Socialist element was kept in the background until the time was more ripe for it. The question was, however, brought to an issue in 1908 by the Osborne case.

Osborne was a railwayman who brought an action against the Railwaymen's Union, of which he was a member, asking for a declaration of the Court of Chancery that a compulsory levy for political purposes was *ultra vires* and illegal. Part of his case was the 'pledge,' exacted from M.P.'s elected through the agency of the Party, that they must abide by its decisions and dissociate themselves entirely from the other parties. This pledge, which completely reversed the attitude of 1901, was adopted in 1903 on the initiative of the I.L.P. It was called a 'declaration of independence,' but since the party was already perfectly free to do as it pleased, the effect, if not the object, was rather to deprive the member of liberty than to give independence to the party. No other party had ever laid down such a condition, the effect of which is to make the member neither the representative of his constituency as a whole nor even of those only who voted for him, nor the exponent of his own opinions, but the paid servant of a caucus.

The law courts decided that a compulsory levy for Parliamentary representation was illegal and that 'an agreement by which a member of Parliament agrees always to vote in a prescribed manner in consideration of certain payments towards his election expenses and support is void as being against public policy.' In pursuance of this decision, finally pronounced in 1909, actions were brought against numerous trade unions and injunctions obtained restraining them from using compulsory levies for political purposes, showing that Osborne represented a large class of aggrieved trade unionists. The Socialists had, in fact, overshot the mark, as the South Wales employers had done before them, and the result was a set-back; membership dropped off, but losses were made good by the accession of the Miners' Federation, which accounted for the seventy-eight candidates and forty members returned in 1910. This, however, meant a relative weakening of the Socialist element, since most of the miners' members were still Liberals.

The Labour Party proceeded to legalise their position by dropping the 'pledge' in 1911, and at the same time the Liberal Government helped them by introducing payment of members. But this was thought insufficient to restore the position they had enjoyed before the Osborne judgment. The unions were perfectly free to have a voluntary political levy, but it was a failure—in itself evidence of the constraint previously exercised; and in 1913 the Trade Union Act was passed legalising a compulsory levy under certain conditions. There must be a resolution of the members by ballot in favour of the levy; the political fund was to be kept separate from others; members unwilling to contribute were to have the right of exemption without forfeiting any other rights. Ballots were taken, but the only details made known are those given by Mr. Beer in his *History of British Socialism.*[1] Down to the end of May 1914, ballots had been taken by sixty-three unions, and the voting figures were 678,063 for, and 407,356 against, the political levy. The noticeable features of this result are the smallness of the aggregate vote, showing a vast number of abstentions, and the comparative size of the dissentient minority. There was evidently no general eagerness for the levy and a strong opposition to it, which has since developed into acute resentment on account of breach of the legal conditions, particularly in regard to exemption.

During the years 1909–1913, when the Labour Party was passing through these trials, the trade unions had turned again to industrial action. Trade was reviving after a depression and the wage-earners, who had suffered a reduction in real wages, naturally and rightly demanded a share in the returning prosperity. At first employers adopted the foolish policy of resisting demands they could afford to concede until a strike took place, when they immediately gave way. The result was an unprecedented outbreak of strikes, culminating in the general coal strike of 1912.

[1] Vol. II, p. 343–4.

These stirring events took attention away from the political movement, and they were accompanied by the importation of Syndicalism, mainly from France, but with a certain American element. A new cry arose, opposed to the Collectivist Socialism of the Fabians and the I.L.P. who were gently steering the Labour Party in their own direction; it is expressed in the phrase: 'the mines for the miners.' The movement was never established on an organised basis, as in France, and made little visible show, but the idea penetrated and exercised far more influence than Socialists were willing to admit. It has indeed permanently modified the whole outlook and is one of the most distinctive features of the third or post-war phase of Socialism. In the period with which we are dealing, it reinforced the effect of the strikes in diverting attention from the political to the industrial field and throwing the Labour Party into the background.

This is in keeping with general experience. In times of rising trade, industrial action comes to the front, in times of depression, recourse is had to the political field. The revival of Socialism in 1880–90 coincided with a period of acute depression, its marked advance in 1900–1905 with another; trade disputes, on the contrary, declined in those periods and rose in the alternate ones, when Socialism was quiescent. By 1913, however, the industrial ferment was becoming exhausted, and its subsidence cleared the way for a revival of political activity.

In 1914, the Labour Party, rehabilitated by the Act of 1913 and the other changes described, passed a resolution on the initiative of the I.L.P., declaring that the aim of the labour movement was to abolish poverty and class oppression by bringing land and industrial capital under the ownership and control of the community for the collective good of all—the old formula of collective Socialism. This may have been intended as a counter-blast to Syndicalism, but at any rate the Socialists in the party must have felt pretty sure of their ground. Similar resolutions had been turned down in 1901 and 1908, though in the latter year a tentative declaration of opinion in favour of socialisation had been adopted by a rather small majority. In general, the astute leaders of the party kept the question in the background, for fear of offending the right wing in the delicately balanced state of opinion; and even in 1914 the mover of the resolution thought it advisable to hedge by declaring that it was not intended to advocate Socialism.

Nevertheless, the resolution did definitely commit the party to Socialism and marked a distinct advance in that direction. Such a declaration by an actual political party with over forty members in Parliament was quite a different thing from the pious expressions of opinion that had for years been passed at the Trades Union Congress, largely because nobody supposed anything would come of them. It had taken thirty years of ceaseless agitation to get so far, such is the massive Conservatism of British workmen. The Co-operative movement, which is sometimes regarded as a branch of Socialism and had a standing invitation to join, remained steadily aloof except for one local society. On the other hand, the socialist and trade union organisations, though remaining independent, had gradually drawn closer together. In 1905, before the momentous election of 1906, a joint board was formed, representing the Trades Union Congress, the General Federation of Trade Unions (a purely industrial body founded in 1899) and the Labour Party.

A distinguishing feature of the campaign for Socialism in this country as compared with the Continent is the use made of meetings and open-air speaking. Meetings are so peculiarly English that the word has been transplanted into other languages, and the 'street-corner' or 'soap-box orator' is a national figure. Elsewhere he is not tolerated by the police. This is counter-balanced by a comparative lack of newspapers. There were weekly papers from 1884 onwards and they gradually increased in number, but it was not until 1912 that a daily paper made its appearance in the *Daily Herald*, followed by the *Daily Citizen*. The former was the official organ of the Labour Party, the latter a private venture. Both led a struggling existence, the one cautious and trade unionist, the other independent and wild. The war increased their difficulties and put an end to the *Daily Citizen*, while the *Daily Herald* became a weekly, returning to the daily issue after the war.

It is a feeble effort compared not only with Germany, but with many little continental countries. Indifference or resistance to Socialism is not the only cause. The mass of the British working classes buy only evening papers containing the latest sport news—racing and football—and Sunday papers devoted to gossip, scandal and crime. There is a certain demand for more informative matter, but the modern tendency is to serve up that too in snippets, whether in newspapers or books. The words 'tit-bits' and 'outlines' characterise the intellectual appetite of this century.

The spread of Socialism has, however, been promoted in recent years by more systematic education in schools for children and colleges for adults. The former are common to many countries, the latter, I believe, peculiar to Great Britain. Sunday schools for teaching Socialism to children were started in 1892, but had not attained large proportions or exercised much influence before the war, though they were then extending rapidly. Socialist colleges came much later. In 1909 a number of students seceded from Ruskin College, Oxford, because the teaching was not revolutionary enough, and founded the first labour college, for the teaching of Marxian economics and history from the same point of view. It moved to London in 1911. Students from this institution, which is supported by the miners and railwaymen's unions in South Wales, exercised considerable influence in the stormy industrial period before the war, always in the direction of promoting strife for revolutionary aims. The celebrated Syndicalist pamphlet, *The Miners' Next Step*, emanated from them. But the full significance of the college and its junior counterpart in Glasgow, as important factors in the situation, belongs to a later period.

Chapter V

THE SECOND PHASE (*Continued*)

Other Countries

The most remarkable fact about the second phase of Socialism was the world-wide distribution of the cult. Gradually in one country after another an organised movement was developed on the same general lines, though with local features, and by 1912 there were some thirty-five on the list, extending from Japan to Chili and from Vancouver to New Zealand. This spread was due in part to the international organisation described in the next chapter, but that would have achieved little without indigenous elements. We have dealt with Germany, France and England, and shown how the revival came about, the forms it took and the progress made. It is neither necessary nor possible to treat the other countries in equal detail; but some account must be given of the more important, if only as an introduction to post-war developments.

Until Bolshevism, which belongs to the third phase, arose, public attention was directed in most countries almost exclusively to their home movement. It certainly was here. In 1909 I wrote a full and detailed account of French Syndicalism, which I had thoroughly studied, not only in Paris, but in most of the large industrial towns of France. That account, which is perfectly valid to-day, was published in *The Times*; but no one took any notice of it, and when Syndicalism made its appearance here two years later, entire ignorance of the subject was revealed by many writers, and particularly by Socialists, who rushed into print with a scanty equipment of second-hand and erroneous information hastily gathered from a book whose author had been misled about the origin and character of the movement. They learnt better in time, but the incident impressed on me the lack of interest in other countries and of desire for knowledge about them. It is indispensable for the student who wishes to understand what is going on now, to take a broad survey, and regard Socialism as a world-wide movement. I will, therefore, give a brief account of those countries which have most claim to notice on various grounds, taking them in chronological order.

SWITZERLAND

The beginning of an organised movement in Switzerland dates from the same period as in Germany; it was, in fact, an off-shoot from Germany started in a small way in 1867. Then the founding of the Marxian party at Eisenach in 1869, described in Chapter III, was followed by the formation of a Social Democratic party in Switzerland in 1870. In 1873 a Labour Association was founded, and in 1878 it adopted principles derived from the German Gotha programme.[1] In 1880 the usual split

[1] Page 57.

occurred, and it was not until 1888 that a united Socialist party was got together, after many unsuccessful attempts at union. Socialism as an effective movement is generally held to date from this step, that is to say from about the same time as in England. But internal dissensions kept it weak, and it made very little progress for many years. In 1904 it adopted a new programme, and in 1905 secured two seats out of 167 in the Swiss Federal Chamber. Those were gradually increased, and became fifteen out of 159 in 1910. Socialism was stronger in the cantonal chambers and municipal councils, particularly in German Switzerland, where its strength always lay. The type is Marxian, of a moderate character. In 1910 the membership of the party was only 21,132 ; trade unionists numbered 131,380 in 1912.

Denmark

This country was first in the field in Scandinavia, and her connection with Germany was the reason. An active campaign, with a newspaper of its own, was started in 1871 by Louis Pio as a branch of the International, and at the same time trade unions were founded under Socialist auspices. Pio's organisation was suppressed in 1873, but in 1878 a Social Democratic party was formed, after a congress held two years before. It revived the former policy of cultivating trade unions, and the two have always been united, forming two wings—political and industrial—of one organisation. This exceptionally intimate connection, together with the development of co-operative societies, gave the movement great strength. In 1884 the party secured two seats in the Lower House of Parliament (Folketing); in 1900 it had twelve, and two seats in the Upper House (Landsting); in 1906 the Socialist members increased to twenty-four in the Lower House and four in the Upper House; in 1913 they secured thirty-two seats in the Lower House. The programme of the party was based on the Erfurt model, but its policy was wholly Reformist.

The peculiarity of Denmark is the great preponderance of the agricultural interest and the large number of small owners and occupiers—two conditions that make for Conservatism in spite of the programmes. The Socialist Press has always been highly developed in Denmark. In 1906 there were twenty-five daily papers, with a circulation of 97,000. The trade unions had a membership of 139,012 in 1912, mostly affiliated to the Socialist Party.

Sweden

Trade unionism preceded Socialism in Sweden, and it assumed a militant type in 1880, after the suppression of a strike in 1879. In 1882 the unions formed a Central Committee with a political as well as an industrial side, and a programme of social and electoral reforms, but in 1885 two Socialist newpapers were started under the influence of Dr. Branting, who has long been one of the most respected and distinguished leaders in Europe, and in 1887 a Social Democratic Labour Party was formed at a Congress, to which all organisations that accepted the principle of the class war were invited. This party was political, but it also took charge of the trade unions, which then had no central organisation of their own; it gave them a head and they gave it a body. In 1897, however, the party authorised the formation of a National Confederation of Trade Unions, and this was effected in 1898. The object was to facilitate the Inter-Scandinavian Labour Movement, which had originated in 1886 and aimed at the co-operation of the three countries in the industrial field. The step involved a certain degree of separation between the political and industrial organisations in Sweden. They were less united than in Denmark, but still worked in close co-operation, as the National Confederation was from the first a Socialist body. The trade unions had, however, no compulsory levy.

The policy of this Social Democratic Party, adopted in 1897, was based on the Erfurt programme, and among other things declared for the abolition of private ownership in land. The party was placed in the dilemma of losing the support of the small land-owners or exempting them from nationalisation, which would in effect involve the abandonment of the Socialist principle. The knot was cut by a revision of the programme in 1911 and the replacement of nationalisation by a pious declaration that the land, like other means of production, ought to be the property of all the workers. The actual policy of the party, however, was Reformist, and particularly directed to franchise reforms; but a revolutionary wing calling themselves Young Socialists was formed from 1906 onwards. The Parliamentary (Second Chamber) progress of the party was—1896, one member (Dr

Branting); 1903, four members; 1906, thirteen; 1909, thirty-three; 1911, sixty-four out of 230. The rapid advance after 1906 was due in part to franchise reforms passed in 1907 and 1909 and partly to the great general strike of 1909, in which the strikers were beaten. An offer by the Radical Prime Minister to take three Socialists into his Cabinet was declined. The total trade union membership in 1912 was 121,866, of whom 85,000 were in the National Federation. After the general strike of 1909, a syndicalist movement for trade union independence of the Socialist Party set in, but it was localised and not important.

Norway

Up till 1905 Norway was constitutionally united with Sweden, though it had a single chamber Parliament of its own, and the history of the Norwegian movement was very similar to the Swedish. It began with the formation of trade unions, which held a Congress in 1880 and appointed a central committee for political purposes in 1884. In 1885 a Social Democratic Federation was founded, and in 1887 a Labour Party, which in 1891 adopted a Socialist programme borrowed from Germany, but for a long time had no electoral success. In 1903 the Socialists secured five seats in the Storthing; in 1906, after separation from Sweden, they rose to ten; in 1909 to eleven; and in 1912 to twenty-three out of one hundred and twenty-three. The relations of the Social Democratic Federation to the trade unions were much the same as in Sweden, but the political levy was compulsory in affiliated unions. The policy of the party was nominally Marxian, but actually Reformist.

Both Sweden and Norway are more industrial and commercial than Denmark, where the agricultural population is 60 per cent. of the whole, and Norway in particular has undergone a rapid industrial development in recent years through the utilisation of water power. In all the Scandinavian countries the rise of Socialism was accompanied by the appearance of daily newspapers supporting the cause, and the number—54 in 1912—is remarkable for so small a population, which only reached an aggregate of ten and a half millions in 1910.

Belgium

The organised movement dates from 1885, when a Labour Party was formed, mainly through the efforts of César de Paepe. The inspiration and the policy were German, but the programme was somewhat modified in 1894. It still retained the class war principle and the aim of converting a capitalist into a collectivist order by nationalising banks, mines, means of production, forests and land; but the administration of public services was to be carried out by autonomous corporations under the control of the State, not by the State itself, and conditions of work were to be settled by conferences between the workmen and the administrative body. The detailed programme of actual reforms was very complete and generally regarded as the best of all the programmes. In 1894 the party gained its first marked electoral success and secured twenty-eight seats in the Chamber of

Deputies, but its subsequent career was chequered and in 1911 it had only advanced to thirty-five members out of 166 in the Chamber and seven out of one hundred in the Senate. It had then eight daily papers and a number of others. The most notable feature of the movement in Belgium is the great development of co-operative societies as part of it, particularly in Flanders. The Socialists have paid more attention to this practical field and to building up trade unions than to politics. The trade union membership in 1912 was 231,535, of whom about half were Socialist. The leader of the party after the death of de Paepe in 1890 was M. Vandervelde, a barrister, who shared with Branting and Jaurès the palm of intellectual distinction among Socialist leaders before the war. Brussels was the seat of the permanent office of the Second International, with Vandervelde for Chairman and Huysmans for Secretary.

Austria

A movement for forming workmen's institutes started in Austria soon after the founding of the Lassallean party in Germany, and in 1869 Liebknecht went to Vienna to preach Marxism ; but the Government suppressed the movement, and it was not until 1888 that the scattered and divided elements representing Socialism came together at a Congress. Dr. Victor Adler, the leader, had started a Socialist paper in 1886. The great demand then was for franchise reform, and years were occupied by agitation on the question. In Austria everything was complicated by the national divisions in that 'ramshackle Empire,' and Socialist organisation among them. But in 1897 the party was reorganised on a basis recognising nationality, and seventeen Socialists were returned to the Reichsrath after a political crisis and a general election under a reformed franchise. After this they fell back, and in 1901 secured only ten seats. But the introduction of adult suffrage in 1906 was followed by a great triumph in 1907, when the Social Democrats polled over a million votes and won eighty-seven seats out of five hundred and sixteen. But once more a set-back followed, and in 1911 they lost five seats. Moreover the party became divided into three groups on a nationality basis—German, Czech and Polish—which did not tend to increase its influence, though they worked together on social questions. Socialism in Austria was successful chiefly in forcing on the franchise reforms and in municipal life, in which it became very strong. The trade union movement was somewhat divided, as Christian unions were formed there, as in Germany, in opposition to the Social Democratic type. The latter had a membership of 428,363 in 1912, out of a total of nearly 700,000.

Italy

The temperament of the Italian people has always inclined them to more violent agitation and more acute dissension than the more Northern peoples previously dealt with, and the history of Socialism in Italy illustrates this tendency. It did not make its appearance there as a defined and organised movement until 1892, when a Congress was held at Genoa, and a Social Democratic party formed on a Marxian basis; but there had been a great deal of confused agitation carried on previously for many years ever since the Russian anarchist, Michael Bakunin, visited the country in 1865 in connection with the First International to preach Anarchism. The conflict between Marx and Bakunin, which tore that organisation to pieces,[1] was carried on with peculiar vehemence in Italy by their respective followers, but the country was too much occupied by war and revolution to pay much attention to such matters until the political situation became more settled after 1871. In 1874 the Government broke up the International section in Italy, where it was thought to be growing dangerous to the new-found national tranquillity, but agitation went on, and the industrial development of Lombardy led to the formation of a workmen's organisation in Milan in 1880. The widening of the franchise in 1881, which brought in the more educated urban workmen, enabled them to return a Socialist member, Andrea Costa, to the Chamber of Deputies in 1882. Ten years later, at the Congress already mentioned, the various groups were brought together into a single party, called the Italian Socialist Party, with the regular Marxian policy of class war and Collectivism. Unity was secured, as in other cases, by ruling out the Anarchists.

The leaders were Antonio Labriola, professor of philosophy, and Filippo Turati, a lawyer and editor of the first Italian Socialist paper, *La Critica Soziale* (weekly), started in 1891. Intellectuals have always

[1] See Chapter VI.

held sway in Italy, and not even in France are movements more closely associated with the personalities of leaders. The united party made rapid progress for some years as the following table shows:

Year	Votes received	Members elected
1892	26,000	6
1897	135,000	16
1900	164,946	32
1904	301,525	23
1910	338,865	40

The Chamber of Deputies consists of 508 members. The population in 1911 was 36 millions and the total number of electors about three millions.

Success in the earlier part of the period brought dissension. The regular division into reformist and revolutionary sections took place in the Marxian ranks, and the anarchists, who had come in again by the back door, raised their heads against both. Turati was the Reformist leader, Ferri, the well-known criminologist, led the dissentient revolutionary section, and Arturo Labriola (not to be confused with Antonio), who had taken up Syndicalism and become one of its most prominent intellectual advocates, guided the anarchists into that congenial camp. In 1904 the growing antagonism between Ferri and Turati came to an issue at the Congress of Bologna, and the latter was defeated. But it made little real difference. As in Germany, the more orthodox Marxians relieved their minds by a victorious declaration of faith, but continued to act as though they did not believe it. Owing to the disposition of political parties, the Socialists were able to exercise considerable influence on reform legislation but in no other way, and whatever their convictions they were in fact Reformists, as everywhere else. In 1910 the fact was recognised and Turati's Reformism approved by a large majority. A much more serious crisis occurred in 1906, when all the Socialist deputies resigned on account of internal dissensions. The sequel was the condemnation of the Syndicalists, who thereupon left the Party and formed a separate organisation.

It has been shown above that the organisation of workmen preceded the formation of the Italian Socialist Party by several years, and trade unionism became strongly developed considering the distribution of the population. The official statistics for 1914 gave the total membership as 971,667; but they were no more united than the Socialists, being organised in several groups, of which one was Catholic and anti-Socialist, as in Germany, Austria and Belgium. A notable fact is the large number of agricultural unions in Italy; they account for nearly half the total membership. It was in the towns, however, and in municipal administration that Socialism was most successful: that form of activity was probably more highly developed in Italy than in any other country. In 1912 the Socialists had a majority in 127 municipalities, and over 3,000 representatives on public bodies. There were four Socialist daily papers, of which the official organ, *Avanti*, was the most important, and 110 weekly journals.

Holland

Organised Socialism appeared late in Holland and made less way there than in any North European country. A Social Democratic Labour Party of the more moderate type was founded in 1894, and in 1897 succeeded in getting three members elected to Parliament in a house of one hundred. They were increased to seven in 1901, but made no further progress at subsequent elections, partly because of internal dissensions, which led to a secession in 1908 and the formation of a more revolutionary rival group calling itself the Social Democratic Party. The latter could weaken the movement but failed to make any way itself; it remained insignificant.

Finland

Socialism came still later to Finland than to Holland, but its progress there presents the greatest possible contrast; for in a short time it outstripped the movement in all other countries. This was probably due to the peculiar political situation of Finland under Russian control, which stimulated the revolutionary ardour of a highly independent people, having no racial affinity with any of their neighbours. The formation of a Labour Party in 1899 followed immediately on the suppression by Russia of the Finnish Constitution; and its efforts were largely responsible for the restoration of local autonomy under a reformed and democratised constitution in 1905. Finland was the first country to adopt female suffrage and admit women to

Parliament. The cause of national freedom brought together all sections of the people in the great general strike of November 1905—the most, if not the only, successful general strike on record. This accounts for the extraordinary success of Socialist candidates in subsequent Parliamentary elections, which were annual under the new constitution. They secured 80 seats out of 200 in 1907, and they rose gradually to 87 (including nine women) four years later, placing the Finnish Labour Party at the head of all Socialist parties in political strength with the sole exception of the Australian. The programme was Marxian and based on the Erfurt pronouncement, but the policy was Reformist and anti-revolutionary. One of the chief activities of the party was the promotion of intellectual culture, in which the Finns, like the Scandinavians, are very advanced. In 1912 the membership of the party was between 50,000 and 60,000 in a population of three millions, but it had six daily papers and many others.

Australia

The case of Australia demands fuller notice than the foregoing. The story of the rise and progress of Socialism there furnishes one of the most remarkable chapters in the whole history of the movement. Here was no old, highly industrialised, congested country, with marked class divisions and social institutions handed down from the past with ancient oppressions, intense competition, small opportunity to rise from the ranks, vast masses of poor contrasted with wealthy idlers. The conditions were just the contrary—a new country possessing immense undeveloped resources, crying out for population, unlimited opportunity, democratic in spirit and in institutions, devoid of class oppression, mainly agricultural, not industrialised, highly prosperous, with little poverty, and no idlers except the work-shy and unemployable. Why should Socialism appear here, and within a space of twenty years acquire far more power than anywhere else? It is a puzzling question to which no single answer can be given. But there is no doubt about the origin of the movement; it was due to propaganda and the personality of one man, William Lane. Born in England, he came in 1883 by way of America to Queensland, where he was a journalist, at first working for a local paper, but before long the owner of a highly successful weekly paper, the *Boomerang*, started by himself in 1885. It was something like the *Clarion* in England and his influence resembled that of Blatchford.

He was an honest enthusiast and a sentimental Socialist fed on Bellamy's *Looking Backward*, an American romance of the Utopian order. Lane addressed himself to the trade unions, which already existed in Australia, but were of a conservative type like the English unions. He set to work to rouse and convert them by his pen, and for that purpose founded another paper, *The Worker*, for their special benefit, with the motto 'Socialism in our time.' He was assisted by various circumstances. The period in which he started this campaign was one of great depression and unemployment, not in Australia, but in England; and emigrants coming out from the old country would be prepared to sympathise with Lane's view and back his efforts. Some were already Socialists, having been members of the Socialist League.[1] The sympathetic connection between the movement in this new country and the old was shown by the fact that the Brisbane unions sent £30,000 to aid the London dockers in the famous strike of 1889, conducted by the 'Strike Kings,' John Burns and Tom Mann, both members of the Social Democratic Federation. Mann went to Australia not long afterwards to carry the torch there. In truth it was a time of general ferment, as the story of other countries told above clearly proves; and in Australia two streams happened to meet, one from America in the person of William Lane, inspired by Henry George and Bellamy, the other from the rising movement in England.

In 1890 Lane had sufficiently prepared the ground for a forward move in Queensland and was able to consolidate the trade union forces into a new central organisation, the Australian Labour Federation, with the object of conquering political power and establishing State collectivism. This was his formula in that year:

> 'The effect of the nationalisation of the means of production and distribution and of the conduct by the State authority of all production and all exchange, would simply be to enable us to produce for use instead of for profit.'

[1] See p. 86.

There is no clearer statement of the principle and purpose of Socialism ; and if the phrase 'conduct by the State authority' be omitted and replaced by 'democratic control' or some such words, it is perfectly modern. One reads precisely the same formula every day. Australian Socialism sprang from the same source as the rest, and events conspired to assist it.

In 1890 occurred the great strike of sheep-shearers, mainly in Queensland. Wool is the great staple product of Australia, and the shearers, who earned high rates of pay, were the strongest body of workmen in the country. It was primarily a labour dispute between employers and employed, but not an ordinary one ; the Australian Labour Federation turned it into a bid for power by direct action. They assumed a sort of dictatorship and took control of the countryside in the areas affected. They issued passports to travellers and held up anyone not provided. Many acts of violence were committed and much property damaged. Troops were called out to protect the pastoralists, but being judiciously handled, they avoided collision with the strikers, many of whom were armed. Eventually the falling of heavy rains and the flooding of the country isolated the strikers and prevented movement. They gave in, and their defeat was promptly utilised by Lane to preach the moral of political action ; the Labour Federation formally adopted the policy of nationalisation and collectivism. The effect was enhanced in the following year by the general shipping strikes, which were an attempt to paralyse the whole trade of the country, including New Zealand, and particularly to prevent the transport of wool. They, too, failed completely, but the victory was dearly bought ; the result was a great impetus to Socialism, which at the next election returned representatives and formed a strong group in all the State legislatures. In 1891 the Socialists won thirty-seven seats in New South Wales, and by 1893 they held eighty seats altogether.

There can be no doubt that the employers by refusing in the first instance to negotiate with the unions on perfectly reasonable wage demands, precipitated this development, which inaugurated the reign of Socialism in Australia. It was the old story of dogged resistance to inevitable change and accomplished fact. On the other hand, the conduct of the strikers alienated public opinion, which had been sympathetic to the shearers ; and the disastrous effects on the trade of the country aroused a general determination to prevent its repetition, which issued in the peculiar Australian system of dealing with disputes. Compulsory arbitration was first adopted in 1893 by New Zealand as an immediate sequel of the shipping strike ; New South Wales followed in 1901, West Australia later, whilst South Australia adopted a mixed system of voluntary and compulsory arbitration, and Victoria preferred wages boards. This movement ran parallel with the development of Socialism, and was much influenced by it. Though compulsory arbitration is to some extent a check on trade union action, it was turned to the advantage of the unions by having compulsory membership associated with it, at the instance of the Socialists, who in return received the support of the unions. So the two worked together.

In 1893 Lane, disillusioned by the conduct of Labour members, who used their newly won power to advance personal interests, left Australia to found an ideal colony on Communist principles in Paraguay. He had always cherished the idea of repeating the experiments of Owen and Cabet, and his sanguine disposition made him confident that he would succeed where they failed. He had every advantage to start with—an excellent and carefully chosen tract of land, ungrudging assistance from the Paraguayan authorities, a picked band of enthusiastic comrades. The venture was a complete failure. Like all the others of the same kind, the experiment of New Australia, as it was called, foundered on the rock of human nature, and once more illustrated the truth of Aristotle's observation that 'there is much more quarrelling among those who have all things in common.' The only exceptions are small communities actuated by intense religious conviction, and wedded to poverty. To adopt Communism with the object of improving economic conditions is like warding off an attack of delirium tremens with a bottle of whisky. Lane, a man of high ideals and lofty character, finding it impossible to carry on New Australia, tried again and founded a second colony called Cosme, about fifty miles away, with a small band of faithful followers. This also failed, and Lane returned to Australia in 1899, but he no longer possessed his former influence. He eventually went to New Zealand, after a visit to England, and took up journalism again. It is clear that the failure of

New Australia was not due to external conditions, because when the remaining colonists went back to ordinary economic life, as they eventually did, they prospered; it was the communistic system that proved unworkable.

Meanwhile, things had changed in Australia. There had been a reaction and the tide of Socialism had ebbed. The establishment of the Commonwealth in 1901 turned men's thoughts in other directions, and the Imperial idea took hold. Appeals for further support and recruits to carry on the Lane schemes met with a cold response. Socialism was represented in the New Parliament, but it was mixed with non-Socialist elements in the Labour group, which in 1904 anticipated recent political events here by being put into office, as a minority, by the other parties. It was the first quasi-Socialist administration to be set up in any country; and that fact alone confers historical distinction upon Australia, which was not merely making an eccentric demonstration, as some supposed, but creating a precedent that has since been followed by the Mother Country, Sweden and Denmark. The Labour Government of 1904 was soon turned out, but the experiment was repeated in 1908, when the Labour groups in the several constituent States were formally federated into one body under the title 'Australian Labour Party.' In 1910 it secured a small majority in both Houses of Parliament, and entered into power as well as office under the premiership of Mr. A. Fisher.

The declared objects of the party were the collective ownership of monopolies and extension of the industrial and economic functions of the

State and municipality—definitely Socialistic, but more Fabian than Marxian. The election programme included nationalisation of monopolies and the establishment of a Commonwealth Bank, but otherwise was either purely Reformist (unemployment insurance, compulsory arbitration, and graduated income tax) or distinctly anti-Socialist (restriction of immigration, a protective tariff). Acts for carrying out the nationalisation of monopolies and compulsory arbitration were passed, but rejected by large majorities on the referendum vote provided for by the constitution. It appears that the Australian electorate were willing to put a Labour Socialist Government in office, but not to take any Socialism from them. Possibly the existence of the referendum, which gives the people ultimate control and is security against freak legislation, had something to do with the Labour majority.

In three of the six Australian States as well as in the Commonwealth Parliament before the war, the Labour Party had a majority in the Lower House and formed the Government; but Queensland, where the movement originated, was not one of them.

In New Zealand, which was involved in the shipping strike of 1891, events took a different course. As already stated, compulsory arbitration in industrial disputes was first adopted there as a sequel of the strike, and the measure is typical of the action adopted in New Zealand, which consisted of drastic restrictive legislation with very little infusion of Socialism proper. Those who called themselves Socialists took up Syndicalism and the general strike, while the Labour group in opposition to them gravitated to a Reformist brand of Socialism, but neither acquired any power. Compulsory arbitration, which is New Zealand's special contribution to the economic problems of the day, proved very unsatisfactory, and in spite of repeated amendments of the original Act, fell into general discredit.

America

The United States presents a striking contrast to Australia. Although it is above all others the land of Capitalism, money power, overgrown industrialism, trusts, millionaires, contrasted poverty and wealth—in short, all the conditions that Socialism exists to combat and abolish—yet there is none in which Socialism, though free and unmolested, has gained so little ground in so long a time. Ever since 1871, when the International [1] was transferred to America in a vain attempt to keep it alive, organised movements of the kind have been carried on there without any solid result. Perhaps one reason is that there have been so many of them. America has presented us with specimens of every species of Labour organisation, from revolutionary anarchist Communism to conservative trade unionism, and they have jostled each other in an extraordinary welter. This is largely due, no doubt, to the mixed population and the cosmopolitan stream of immigrants. But there

[1] See Chapter VI.

is a peculiar instability about things in the States; organisations appear, wax, wane and disappear or change. Trade unionism has shared this tendency with Socialism, which it long preceded.

As far back as 1834 there was a National Trades Union. Little is known about it, but it does not appear to have lasted long. Later we find a series of ambitious attempts to found general organisations, to include the sectional unions or supersede them—National Labour Union (1866), Knights of Labour (1869), Sovereigns of Industry (1874), Industrial Brotherhood, (1874), American Federation of Labour (1881), American Labour Union (1902), Industrial Workers of the World (1905), Workers' International Industrial Union (1915). Besides these and variously related to them are several federations of trade unions—miners, railwaymen, metal workers, engineers and others. The Socialist bodies have been still more numerous—Social Party (1868), International Workingmen's Association (1871), Social-Democratic Workingmen's Party of North America (1874), Workingmen's Party of the United States (1876), Socialist Labour Party (1877), International Working People's Association (1883 Anarchist), Socialist Trades and Labour Alliance (1895), Social-Democratic Party (1898), Socialist Party (1901). The relations between these bodies form a jig-saw puzzle which it is not worth while to put together; only two bodies representing Socialism and two trade unionist federations need fuller consideration. These are the Socialist Labour Party and the Socialist Party on the one hand; the American Federation of

Labour and the Industrial Workers of the World on the other.

The Socialist Labour Party was formed in 1877 by merging three antecedent bodies and for some time it held the field. It was rigidly Marxian, of the revolutionary class war type, uncompromisingly opposed to all Reformism and to existing trade unionism, which it attempted to supersede by a new revolutionary industrial organisation. This idea, which anticipated the 'industrial unionism' or 'greater unionism' or the 'one Great Union' advocated here much later by some of our more voluble intellectuals, took shape in the Socialist Trades and Labour Alliance (1895)—a body bearing much the same relation to the Socialist Labour Party that the 'Red International of Labour Unions' bears to-day to the Communist International of Moscow. It was an attempt to organise workmen under Socialist control and enrol them in the army of revolutionary Marxism. The author of the scheme was David de Leon, a German Jew whose real name was Loeb, the leader of the Socialist Labour Party. His position in regard to both bodies corresponded precisely with that of Zinovieff in regard to their Bolshevist counterparts. The attempt failed. The S.T. and L.A. was the sickly child of a none too robust parent, and never grew up. The parent itself, the S.L.P., never gained any strength worth mentioning, and gradually wasted away. Its political influence is shown by the number of votes cast for the candidate whom it ran with more courage than discretion at successive presidential elections: 1872, 21,572; 1896, 36,275; 1900, 34,191; 1904, 33,536; 1908, 13,825. The total votes cast at these elections were twelve millions in 1872 and fifteen and a half millions in 1908, from which the hold obtained by unadulterated Marxism in America can be gauged.

The Socialist Party came into the world much later than the foregoing and did much better. Originally it called itself the Social Democratic Party (1898) but changed its name in 1901. Its principles were Marxian, but its policy was Reformist, approximating to that of the English I.L.P. It grew pretty quickly and by 1912 had about 100,000 members. From 1900 onwards it ran a candidate of its own for the Presidency with the following result in votes: 1900, 96,931; 1904, 409,230; 1908, 424,483. It made a much better showing than its rival, though the total is insignificant. The figures indicate a growing influence, which was emphasised at the Congressional and State elections in 1910. In the former the party polled an aggregate of 607,674 votes and had one of its leaders, Victor Berger, elected to the House of Representatives for Milwaukee—the first Socialist to enter Congress. In the State elections they did still better, securing a total of 17 seats in different States. Milwaukee (a German town) was fairly captured by Socialists, and the example was followed by a considerable number of towns, in later elections, mainly in the West. In the stormy strike years before the war Socialist representation in State legislatures and municipalities grew apace.

Nevertheless, Socialism remained peculiarly weak in the United States, largely because of its relations with trade unionism, which are quite different from those in any of the countries hitherto discussed.

Both the trade union organisations mentioned above have been more or less openly hostile, but for different reasons. The American Federation of Labour, which is by far the larger of the two, and the really effective body in America, has consistently maintained the chief characters of English unionism before that fell under Socialist influence—the craft basis, the principle of self-help, defence of workmen's interests in the industrial field, avoidance of politics, non-revolutionary tactics, methods of agreement and conciliation with employers—in short, everything that is called reactionary in the revolutionary camp. This is due in a great measure to the commanding personality of the president Samuel Gompers, a Londoner by birth, of Jewish parentage, who died in December, 1924. American employers did not love him, and he was at one time prosecuted for his trade union activities; but Socialists loved him less, for the American Federation of Labour under his influence has been a great stumbling-block in their way. Founded in 1881 it soon superseded the waning Knights of Labour and other attempted central organisations; and in 1912, when the total trade union membership in the United States was returned at 2¼ millions (German *Statistisches Jahrbuch*), it accounted for nearly two millions.

The other trade union federation, the Industrial Workers of the World, familiarly known as 'the Wobblies,' was founded in 1905 by the amalgamation of several Socialist and trade union elements, dissatisfied with the inaction of existing bodies. In that respect it may be said to have resembled the English I.L.P., but in no other. The idea in the mind of the organisers is revealed in the letter of invitation to the inaugural meeting, which expressed 'confidence in the ability of the working class, if correctly organised on both political and industrial lines, to take possession of and operate successfully the industries of the country.' This attempted union of the political and industrial policies reflects the dual composition of the new body, but the elements proved unable to hold together and soon split up. They were, indeed, united only by a common opposition to Capitalism and the American Federation of Labour, which was violently attacked from the first; in other respects there were all sorts of divisions between them, both of personalities and principles, and no clear policy or firm leadership. It is not surprising that the I.W.W. inspired little confidence and that the anticipated defections from the American Federation of Labour did not take place; such as did were neither large nor lasting. At the end of a year the paid up membership, nominally 60,000, was only 14,000; and when the Western Federation of Miners seceded in the following year, the I.W.W. lost the only solid support it had. Anarchist and Socialist leaders fought angrily for the control of a machine that broke down at the start.

In 1908, only three years from its foundation, the organisation split completely into two halves—a political and an industrial half—the former was really the old Marxian Socialist Labour Party under another name; the latter became a purely Syndicalist body, resembling the French General Confederation in aims and methods, but not in organisation. This is the I.W.W. known to popular fame, which has invented various sarcastic readings of the initials—I Want Whisky, I Won't Work, International Wonder Workers, etc. It owed nothing to French inspiration, but was a spontaneous American growth; it took up and developed industrial unionism and direct action that had previously existed in some mining valleys. Syndicalism is, in truth, a natural trade union inference from the doctrine underlying Socialism, that Labour (in the narrow sense) produces all the wealth, and so long as that doctrine is taught to trade unionists some will always draw the inference for themselves—if we produce all wealth, then let us take it without more ado.

The Syndicalist I.W.W., which had its seat in Chicago, and was much stronger than its Socialist rival, acted up to its principles and engaged on a great campaign of strikes, marked by violence and lawlessness, particularly in the year 1912–13. After that it suffered a decline, but came up again during the War. Numerically a small body, not approaching the French General Confederation in size, it has been exceedingly active in agitation. Between this skirmishing type of trade unionism and the big battalions of the American Federation of Labour, Socialism has been squeezed tight; for though they are in deadly opposition to each other, they are equally hostile to Socialism.

It only remains to add that the I.W.W. has not confined its activities to the United States, but has extended them to Canada, Australia, South Africa and Great Britain, though with very little success. With regard to the general position in Canada, it is sufficient to say that the labour movement there has always had much in common with that of the States. Both the American trade unions and the Socialist organisations have endeavoured to treat the whole continent as one. The word 'international' in this connection generally signifies the inclusion of Canada. Nevertheless the Canadians have, in the main, gone their own way, and have proved even more resistant to Socialism than the Americans. In 1911 one Socialist was elected to Parliament for Vancouver, which was then the chief stronghold. The prevailing type of Socialism was the revolutionary Marxian, but the usual rival groups made their appearance and spent such small strength as they possessed in combating each other.

I have now given an account of sixteen out of the thirty-three countries represented at the last regular International Congress held in 1910. Russia is better dealt with later under the head of Bolshevism. The rest, which include the Balkan States, the Peninsula, Armenia, Persia, the Far East and South America, do not call for notice. They present no particular features, except, perhaps, the marked tendency to Anarchism in the Peninsula. Otherwise, their Socialism presents the same characteristics in an earlier stage of development.

The most remarkable facts that emerge from the story are the world-wide spread and growing strength of the movement, the general adoption of the Marxian or German formula, but the divergence from it in practice, the consequent division into Reformist and Revolutionary sections, the incessant discussions and irresistible tendency to secession and the formation of fresh groups, leadership by intellectuals but dependence on organised labour for success, the consequent efforts of rival groups to capture the trade unions or create them. These features are constantly reproduced in varying degrees.

To complete the history it is necessary to review the international organisation which has accompanied the developments described.

Chapter VI

INTERNATIONAL SOCIALISM

Socialism, as a movement for the economic reorganisation of society, necessarily has an international outlook because the conditions it desires to transform are common to all civilised countries, though in different stages of development. Any country which adopted it alone would be left in isolation, as Russia is to-day, and we can see the difficulties that arise in consequence. They are one of the reasons for the persistent endeavours of the Moscow Government to make other nations follow their example. It is indeed obvious that any people who establish and carry on their economic activities on an entirely different basis from their neighbours cannot do business with them so easily as if they were both on the same economic basis, and if the difference be fundamental they may be unable to do it at all.

Such a fundamental difference is that between legal recognition and denial of the rights of private property. This does not seem to have been perceived as a general proposition, probably because the contingency has never been thought possible; but it is clear enough and we have witnessed its working in the attempts to deal with Bolshevist Russia. The rulers of that country have been forced by the logic of facts to modify their economic system, but they have not modified it sufficiently to be on the same footing as the rest of the world, and until they do, their economic relations with other countries will never go smoothly. A perfectly self-contained community is independent and can have what system it pleases, but those which depend on economic intercourse with others must not diverge too far from the common practice and the recognised rules. This is one of the reasons for the invariable failure of communistic settlements, even when they have not been destroyed by internal dissensions.

Socialists have never explicitly recognised this obstacle to the realisation of their aims, but they have always instinctively felt that the transformation they contemplate must be world-wide. The idea was not invented by Marx; it found repeated expression during the first phase of Socialism described in Chapter II, and may be said to have been common, implicitly or explicitly, to all the schools. Two or three examples will suffice. At the weekly meeting of the National Union of the Working Classes [1] held on August 17th, 1831, an address to the people of Ireland, was adopted in which the following passage occurred:

> 'We hope the day is not distant when the oppressed poor of every country will unite in sentiment and action for the benefit of the whole human race.' [2]

William Lovett, writing on the Working Men's

[1] See p. 29. [2] *Poor Man's Guardian*, 20th August, 1831.

Association, which was a successor of the above society formed in 1836 and the standard bearer of Chartism, says he believed it had 'the honour of first introducing the mode of *international addresses* between the *working-men* of different countries'; and he quotes an address issued to the Working Classes of Belgium in November 1836, pointing out that the foolish dissensions between nations were due to the ignorance of the working classes, who failed to realise their real position in society—'that we, being *the producers of wealth, have the first claim to its enjoyment*'—and that emancipation would depend on the spread of this knowledge 'among the working-classes of all countries,' and which would lead to the general adoption of the principles laid down by the authors of the Address for the reconstruction of society. An eloquent reply was received from the Working Men of Belgium, signed by Committees at Brussels, Ghent and Liége.[1]

In France the idea found simultaneous and independent expression. The same year, 1831, in which the National Union voted the address to Ireland, quoted above, witnessed also the official statement of the Saint-Simonian doctrine drawn up by Bazard and Enfantin. This document, after deploring the prevalence of strife and antagonism in Europe, went on to indicate a bond of union among men which would lead them towards a common destiny and 'give society, the globe itself, the entire world a character of union, wisdom and beauty.' The science of history, according to Saint-Simon, revealed an irresistible tendency

[1] *Life and Struggles of William Lovett* Chapter V.

towards 'universal association,' and those words figured prominently in the heading of *Le Globe*, the official organ of the school, as its grand aim.

When, therefore, Marx concluded the Communist Manifesto (1848) by calling on the workers of the world to unite, he was broaching no new idea, though his application of it to the class war was his own. As already related nothing came of that at the time, but Marx continued to cherish the idea and in 1864 took advantage of a trade union movement in London, where he resided, to put it on an organised basis in the shape of the 'International Association of Working Men,' which afterwards became known as the First or Old International. The said trade union movement was connected with the Exhibition of 1862. It has already been mentioned in connection with the origin of German Socialism[1] that a party of German workmen from Berlin came to London to visit the Exhibition. A party of French workmen did so too, and their visit, which was promoted by the French Emperor, was repeated in the following year, when the Polish question was discussed. They foregathered with English colleagues and were entertained by others interested in trade unionism and labour questions. In this way the international idea was fostered until the time seemed ripe for a definite organisation to develop it.

So in 1864 the International Association was born. Two real Labour men, George Odger and Robert Applegarth, were employed as midwives to bring the infant to birth, but Marx was the

[1] See p. 53.

physician in charge, who directed the proceedings, and Professor Beesly stood sponsor. The trade unions in general stood rather stiffly aloof, and if that was so in England the labour element had still less part in the organisation on the Continent, where trade unionism hardly existed. The name of the Association was, in fact, deceptive. It was not an Association of workmen but an attempt to get workmen to adopt Marx's theories. It consisted of a central body called the General Council with local branches in the affiliated countries. The Council, which had its seat in London, was internationally constituted, with delegates from the several national branches. It had no authority, but acted as medium of communication and arranged congresses, which took place annually in the four years 1866–69.

As indicated in the previous chapter, it had a good deal to do with starting organised Socialism in several countries, and it promoted the development of the movement in all. This accounts for the stereotyped pattern. The main function of the Association was educational; it was an institute for the propagation of Marxism. "We may observe," says Professor Sombart, "how at each congress of the International Association, there showed itself a gradually strengthening influence of the Marxian spirit." The result was strife. "For as soon as the I.A. showed signs of being Marxian to any degree, disagreements arose in all directions."[1] First the Proudhonian Socialists, then the trade unions and then the German Lassalleans grew restive in turn. But the crowning quarrel

[1] Werner Sombart: *Socialism and the Social Movement.*

which split the I.A. was that between Marx and Bakunin.[1]

The two were old acquaintances from the days of the revolutionary forties, but they never got on well together. Bakunin started out from the philosophy of Hegel, like Marx, Lassalle, Liebknecht, Hess, Ruge, and all the other German intellectuals ; but he took the turning that leads to extreme individualism, and association with Proudhon converted this into anarchism. But his anarchism was quite different from Proudhon's, which was wholly pacific ; Bakunin's was wholly destructive ; probable because of his Russian experiences. He was, in fact, the first anarchist in the ordinary sense of the word, and all later demonstrations of the doctrine can be traced to him. He left a trail behind him everywhere in his many wanderings after his escape from Siberia, notably in Italy and Spain, where the soil was most congenial. Russia he could not enter, but his teaching could, and it took deep root there. It played a part in all the subsequent revolutionary movements, which culminated in Bolshevism.

The quarrel with Marx was fought out in the International. In 1868 Bakunin, who had been actively engaged in propaganda for several years, founded a rival 'International Alliance of Social

[1] Michael Bakunin (1814–1876). Russian aristocrat by birth and officer in the Russian army ; resigned his commission and joined a students' class in Moscow ; in 1841 went to Germany, studied philosophy with the young Hegelians in Berlin and Dresden ; went to Paris and met French Socialists ; met German Communists in Switzerland ; returned to Paris in 1847 ; expelled from France in 1848, took leading part in revolutionary rising in Dresden, handed over to Russian authorities in 1851, exiled to Siberia in 1855, escaped in 1861, came to England by way of America ; spent the rest of his life preaching anarchism in different countries and opposing Marx.

Democracy,' but it was still-born, and he, with his followers, joined the I.A.W.M. Then came the Franco-German War which knocked International Socialism on the head for the time being and caused the seat to be nominally transferred to New York. Before it could recover from the blow the Marx-Bakunin struggle gave it a finishing stroke from within at a congress held in 1872 at the Hague, when the Bakunin party was expelled. The representatives of the Lassallean party who had been present, reported to their own annual meeting that the Hague Congress had been deliberately packed to give Marx a majority; and it is certain that he attached great importance to the occasion because both he and Engels attended in person. After this a feeble attempt was made to hold a Congress at Geneva in 1873; but the thing was dead, and a belated funeral oration was pronounced in 1876.

Such was the First International. It made a great stir and alarmed many ruling statesmen including Bismarck, though it did nothing but give resonance to the doctrines of Marx. Sombart calls it the first agency for the propagation of Marxian teaching, and that was precisely the object for which it was created. But there was no substance in it, and when it came close to any practical question, it revealed irreconcileable differences of opinion or sheer futility. An instance of the former was its enthusiastic support of the Paris Commune in 1871, which completely alienated the English section. An instance of the latter was its behaviour towards the Austro-German War of 1866 and the Franco-German War of 1870.

The most interesting thing in the history of

International Socialism is, indeed, its relation to war. By its very nature it must be opposed to war, which sunders nations vertically and unites classes within them, for its own object is exactly the contrary. It seeks to unite nations vertically and split each horizontally in order to carry on the class war in all. In short, war between nations is its negation. Accordingly, the I.A.W.M. tabulated an emphatic condemnation of the Austro-German war and protested against the Franco-German war, but made not the slightest attempt to prevent either.

In connection with the Franco-German War, a very interesting episode, bearing on recent events, is related by Hermann Wendel, in a memoir written for the German working classes on the occasion of the death of Bebel in 1913. All Germany was hurrahing for the war in 1870, and the Socialists with the rest, excepting Bebel and Liebknecht, who considered the position seriously in the light of their principles. They were members of the North German Reichstag, which had been convened to vote the war loan. Liebknecht intended to vote flatly against it ; but during an enforced wait of several hours at a railway station on their way, Bebel persuaded him to adopt a 'more correct attitude.' This was revealed in the debate of July 21st, 1870, when they declared that :

> 'They could neither vote for the loan, as that would be equivalent to a vote of confidence in the Prussian Government, *which had prepared for the present war by the proceedings of* 1866, nor could they by refusing the required credit

appear as though they approved of the wicked and treacherous policy of Bonaparte. As opponents on principle of every dynastic war, as Socialist Republicans and members of the International Workmen's Association, which fights against all oppressors without distinction of nationality and seeks to unite all the oppressed in a great fraternal band, they could neither directly nor indirectly declare themselves in favour of the present war and would, therefore, abstain from voting . . .'

A lame and impotent conclusion. The declaration, which was inscribed in the journals of the House is typical. Bebel also recounts the incident in his autobiography, but at the same time gives an explanation of the origin of the war at variance with the passage about Bonaparte's policy, which was given as a reason for not voting against the war-loan.

'Liebknecht,' he says, 'believed in the Emperor Napoleon's responsibility for the war. I was of a different opinion, being convinced that Napoleon had fallen into a trap prepared for him by Bismarck.

'To-day there can be no doubt that the war of 1870 was desired by Bismarck and that he had long laid his plans to bring it about. . . . With the exception of a small inner circle of intimates who knew that he had worked with might and main to bring about the war—and not even the King of Prussia belonged to this inner circle—he duped the whole world, making everyone believe that Napoleon had provoked the war and that poor peace-loving Bismarck was the aggrieved party. The historians, official and semi-official, have fostered this belief among the mass of the people—the belief that Germany acted in defence, and that France was the aggressor. It is true that Napoleon declared war, but the master stroke of Bismarck's policy was that he shuffled the cards in such a way that Napoleon was forced to declare war, as though of his own accord, and to play the part of peace-breaker. Even men like Marx and Engels shared the common opinion and gave public expression thereto, although in their position they ought to have known better. The events that preceded the declaration of war were so confusing and unexpected that people quite overlooked the fact that France, who declared war, was quite unprepared, while Germany had all her preparations completed to the last button, and succeeded in mobilising her forces without the slightest hitch.'[1]

Yet there had been meetings of Socialists both in Paris and in German towns and resolutions had been passed against war; but when it came to the point they vanished into smoke. Wendel, who took Bebel's view of the war and Bismarck's responsibility for it, describes the popular excitement in Germany as greater even than in the revolutionary year 1848. 'Not only on every hurdy-gurdy but in every heart rang out the 'Wacht am Rhein,' on

[1] A. Bebel: *My Life*, pp. 205–6.

every hill-top blazed the sacrificial fires of patriotic enthusiasm.'

After this it is not surprising that the First International went under. Nor was it until 1889 that its successor was established, and even then in inauspicious circumstances. According to Mr. Adolphe Smith, who acted as an official interpreter at all the congresses of the Second International, the foundation was laid at an International Conference held in Paris in 1882. Other meetings followed, and as 1889 approached suggestions were made in many quarters for a great congress in Paris to celebrate the centenary of the French Revolution. At once the rivalry between the Socialist parties in France broke into open conflict for the control of the proposed Congress. The British Trades Union Congress invited delegates to a preliminary meeting in 1888, at which it was decided to support the moderate or Reformist French party and entrust them with the arrangements for the Congress. But the Marxians also found support at another preliminary conference held at the Hague. So the result was that two rival Congresses were held in 1889. German Socialists dominated the Marxian one, English trade unionists were conspicuous in the other.

The Second International was thus born amid great confusion and a hubbub of conflicting opinions. It may be regarded as a climax to the active, varied and discordant movements that had been going on for some years both on the trade union and the Socialist side in England, France and other countries in this fermentative period, as described in Chapters

[1] Hermann Wendel: *August Bebel*, p. 41.

IV and V. However, it struck the promoters that the simultaneous holding of rival Congresses was not a very auspicious way of inaugurating a new movement for uniting men in one brotherhood and it was arranged that the next Congress, held in Brussels in 1891, should be a joint affair. This was done without a rupture, but so strong were the antagonisms that it was found impossible to reconcile all shades of opinion ranging in a long scale from trade unionism to anarchist communism. The question was where to draw the line, and at the third Congress, held at Zürich in 1893, the majority agreed to draw it at the anarchists and advocates of physical force, who were accordingly expelled. A common hostility to the extreme left drew the other sections together, in accordance with the universal law of human nature that the most powerful influence in uniting men is a common enemy, or that differences are most easily reconciled in the presence of greater differences. The same question was raised again at the next Congress held in London in 1896 and the previous decision was upheld, though considerable disagreement manifested itself.

Up to this time four Congresses had been held with an increasing membership, but there was no standing organisation and the whole thing was carried on in a very loose way. The principles of the socialisation of the means of production and political action were upheld, but the practical policy, if any, was of a reformist character and reflected the influence of the union and moderate Socialist elements. But at the fifth Congress, held in Paris in 1900, steps were taken to put the organisation on a firmer basis and to define its objects with greater precision. A permanent office was set up in Brussels and an Executive Committee appointed, consisting of two representatives from each national delegation and one from the Socialist Parliamentary Party in each country. M. Vandervelde was Chairman and M. Huysmans Secretary of the International Socialist Bureau so constituted. Along with this development of organising machinery the Congress formulated the principles of the International on regular Marxian lines—the proletariat, enslaved working class, capitalist organisation of production, socialisation of means of production, class war. 'Social democracy has taken upon itself the task of organising the proletariat into an army ready for the social war and it must, therefore, above all ensure that the working classes become conscious of their class interests and of their strength. To this end it must adopt every possible measure and advocate every possible reform.'

The means suggested were participation in political life, universal suffrage, organisation in political, trade union and co-operative groups, workingmen's educational societies. All this was already very familiar in 1900, but it is interesting as an indication of the ideas then prevailing, to the exclusion of Syndicalism and revolutionary action; it might be described as Marxism with a Fabian twist. The resolution embodying the principles was passed with one dissentient.

Still more interesting, however, was the decided attitude to war taken up by the Congress. Previous Congresses had discussed and condemned militarism, but the question had not been made so prominent or handled with so much decision before. Jaurès, who presided, struck the note in his opening address, for which he received the official thanks of the German Government. He denounced the capitalism of that date for 'seeking to maintain its position by stirring up old race prejudices and by inciting one people against another,' and declared that 'the most important question on their agenda was the organisation of peace and international brotherhood.' In pursuance of this pronouncement the Congress unanimously adopted a resolution enjoining Socialists in every country to oppose militarism and colonial expansion with increased energy and demanding an alliance of the proletarians of all lands for the perpetuation of peace, not by mere platonic demonstrations of international solidarity but by 'energetic international action.' Three practical means were recommended: (1) The rising generation to be educated against militarism, (2) Socialist members of Parliament always to vote against any expenditure on the army, the navy or colonial expeditions, (3) the Executive Committee to organise simultaneous, uniform protests in all countries whenever occasion called for them.

The position so defined in 1900 was re-affirmed at the seventh Congress held at Stuttgart in 1907, where it formed the chief item on the programme. A long resolution was adopted, beginning with the usual assertion of the responsibility of capitalism for wars, and continued:

'Wars are therefore the very marrow of

capitalism and will cease with the suppression of the capitalist system or else when the magnitude of the sacrifice in men and money demanded by the development of military technique and revulsion against armaments shall force the people to abandon that system. . . . For these reasons the Congress deems it the duty of all workers and their parliamentary representatives to oppose naval and military armaments with all their might—thereby emphasising the class character of bourgeois society and the motives which impel it to maintain national antagonisms —and to refuse all financial support to that policy. . . .

'The International cannot lay down in advance fixed plans of action, which must necessarily vary for different countries according to time and circumstances; but its duty is to intensify and co-ordinate as far as possible the efforts of the working class against militarism and war. The Congress declares that if a war threatens to break out it is the duty of the working classes in the countries affected, and the duty of their parliamentary representatives with the assistance of the International, to take concerted action and do their utmost to prevent war by all the means which seem to them appropriate and which naturally vary according to the intensity of the class war and the general political situation. In case war breaks out nevertheless, it is their duty to intervene to bring it promptly to an end and to utilise with all their might the economic and political crisis created by the war in order to *stir up the lowest sections of the population* (*agiter les couches populaires les plus profondes) and precipitate the overthrow of the capitalist régime.'*

The last sentence, which I have italicised, has an instructive bearing on post-war events; advantage was to be taken of war to foment a revolutionary agitation amongst the lowest classes of the community. But the main point is the prevention of war, and the striking feature of the resolution is the contrast between the emphatic terms in which the duty of Socialists is laid down and the extremely vague ones referring to the form it should take. Some delegates, and notably the French ones, felt this and wished to go much farther. They proposed to lay down definite measures, such as strikes, desertion by soldiers and refusal of duty; but the Congress, at which Germans preponderated, refused to adopt this course.

The vague resolution, which committed the members to nothing, was a German formula, drafted by Bebel. He was sincere in his opposition to war and had suffered for his opinions; but he was, as I have said before, essentially a politician and an opportunist. At the annual meeting of the German Social Democratic Party at Jena in 1905 he had enthusiastically defended the general strike as a Socialist weapon, in opposition to the opinion of the trade unions, that it was not an arguable proposition; but a few months later in a Conference between the party and the trade unions he took exactly the opposite line and declared that the leaders of the Party did not intend to advocate the general strike, but would as far as possible endeavour to prevent anything of the kind. The question came up at the annual meeting of the Party in 1906 and caused a very lively debate. Bebel endeavoured to reconcile his previous inconsistent utterances by saying that though he had recommended the general strike as a weapon in the last resort he did not mean that they should use it at once; and he particularly opposed a resolution that a general strike should be called to prevent Germany from intervening in the revolutionary struggle going on in Russia. He thought Germany would not intervene. If she did it would mean a European war, and the proposal to call a general strike on behalf of peace on the outbreak of war was puerile.

> 'Who believes that at a moment when a violent shock, a fever, is stirring up the masses to their lowest depths, when the perils of a gigantic war and its appalling misery confront us—who believes that at such a moment it is possible to institute a general strike? From the first day of the outbreak of such a war there march under arms in Germany five million men, with many hundreds of thousands of Socialists among them. The entire nation is in the ranks. Frightful want, universal unemployment, starvation, stoppage of industries, fall of securities—is it credible that at such a moment, when each is thinking of himself, a general strike could be declared?'

All very true, but very different from what was said at Jena the year before, and from the impression left at Stuttgart the year after. Bebel's resolution there adopted gave the impression that the Germans would go to any lengths to prevent war, but actually left them free to do as little as they pleased. M. Vandervelde wrote an article on this congress for *The Times* (September 12th, 1907), which showed that he was hoodwinked. He admitted the disagreement between the German and French members, but minimised it and excused the vagueness of the German attitude by the difficulties of their position. He thought the terms of the resolution might have been clearer and more precise, but took an optimistic view and fortified it with a characteristic remark made by Victor Adler, the Austrian leader:

> 'We Germans are not fond of empty threats We prefer to go farther than our promises. We cannot, and will not, say what we should do if the case arose, but you may rely upon it we should act with as much energy as anyone else.'

They did; in support of an aggressive war against Serbia, involving the deliberate destruction, without any provocation whatever, of M. Vandervelde's own country.

The comedy was repeated at Copenhagen in 1910, when the next Congress, and the last regular one, was held. This congress was attended by 887 delegates, representing thirty-three nations, which shows the great extension of the movement. The last regular congress of the First International in 1869 had been attended by 80 delegates, representing nine nations, the first united congress of the Second International in 1891 by 350 delegates, representing twelve nations. A comparison of these figures with 1910 shows how great the advance had been, but increased size did not prevent the Second from crumpling up even more completely than the First, when put to the test of reality. The other Socialists should have been warned of what was coming by the conduct of the German comrades. At Stuttgart, they had opposed the French demand for more definite action against war; at Copenhagen, the same demand was pressed by the British delegates with French support, but again the Germans successfully opposed it.

Yet two years later one more effort was made, and matters were carried a little farther. This was at a special congress in 1912, called in view of the Balkan crisis under the banner of 'War Against War.' It met at Basel in Switzerland, and was attended by 555 delegates, representing all the principal European countries. The Congress unanimously adopted a long manifesto which recited the Stuttgart and Copenhagen resolutions, but was novel and interesting in that it laid specific commands on the Socialists of the several countries in turn. The Balkan comrades were to compose old enmities, oppose violation of the rights of others and declare the fraternity of all the Balkan peoples. The Austrians were to continue their energetic opposition to any attack on Serbia, and strive to secure self-government for the Southern Slavs. The Austrians and Italians were to oppose every attempt to draw Albania within the sphere of their influence, the Russians were to fight Tsarism and all military policies; but the most important task was laid on Germans, French, and British. They were to insist that their Governments should refuse all support to Austria and Russia, keep out of the Balkans, and maintain a strict neutrality.

After some more injunctions of the same kind, the manifesto concluded with the stereotyped formula about the capitalist world of exploitation and murder, and the proletarian world of peace and union among the nations. A Belgian Socialist, writing of this manifesto in 1915, called it an ironical parody of the history of actual events put in the form of a prophecy: for the proletariat, in whose name the International professed to speak, proceeded to back their respective Governments in exactly the opposite course to that undertaken. The Balkan peoples, for whose benefit the Congress was primarily summoned, promptly set to work to cut each other's throats with all the old zest; and the blame can hardly be put on capitalism at large, for they are the least capitalistic of European States.

In the same year (1913), the German Socialists, who had always dominated the International, were put to the test at home. The German Government, then preparing for the war of 1914, proposed a large increase of the standing army. The Socialists issued a pamphlet denouncing the proposal, admitting that the new French Army Act was only the consequence of German measures, and declaring that though they were in favour of a defensive national militia, they would grant nothing for the class army of militarism: 'Not a single uniform button.' What they did in the Reichstag was to vote against the Army Increase Bill, but for the Finance Bill which provided the money for it. They were rather apologetic at the annual meeting that year, which was their jubilee, but maintained that they had done what they could—had not Comrade Noske made a speech of four and a half hours?—and hinted that if more support were forthcoming from the rank and file, they could do more. However, the fact remains that after swearing they would never consent to provide a single button, they consented to provide everything.

The turn of the Austrian Socialists came with the approach of war in 1914. What did they do? On the eve of war they issued a pamphlet, in which they repudiated all responsibility for war, and argued that there was not sufficient reason for it, but rather defended the Austrian ultimatum to Serbia, and hinted that the way to avoid war was for Serbia to comply. That was how Dr. Adler's boast at Stuttgart was fulfilled. Three days later (28th July), the German Socialists issued a manifesto which took quite a different line and may be commended to the attention of the industrious white-washers of Germany and Austria.

'While we condemn the intrigues of Pan-Serbian nationalism, the frivolous provocation to war by the Austro-Hungarian Government calls for our most energetic protests. The demands of this Government have a brutality unprecedented in the history of the world as addressed to an independent nation and can be intended only to provoke war. The conscious proletariat of Germany, in the name of humanity and civilisation, raises an impassioned protest against the criminal intrigues of the war-mongers. It imperatively demands of the German Government to use its influence on the Austrian Government for the maintenance of peace, and if the horror of war cannot be prevented, that it will have nothing to do with the conflict.'

Two days earlier the *Vorwärts* had denounced the Austrian Government and added:

'There is not the least doubt that the (German) Chancellor has promised his support to Count Berchtold. The game played at Berlin is as dangerous as that played at Vienna.'

Meantime, the International Bureau had called a special anti-war meeting which was held in Brussels on July 29th, and was attended by representatives of Germany, Austria, France, England, Italy, Belgium, Switzerland and others. It was decided, on the motion of the German delegates, to advance the date of the next full Congress, which was to have been held in Vienna on August 23rd, and to hold it instead in Paris on August 9th, and meantime it was the duty of the proletarians of all the countries concerned to intensify their demonstration against war and in favour of referring the Austro-Serbian dispute to arbitration. Those of Germany and France were to put more pressure than ever upon their respective Governments, the one to exercise a moderating influence on Austria, the other to induce Russia to keep out of the conflict. Haase, for Germany, made a particularly interesting speech. He said:

> 'Austria has for five and twenty years aimed at the economic strangulation of Serbia. The ultimatum was therefore in reality a regular provocation to a war willed and desired. The reply of Serbia was, as we all know, composed in such a spirit of moderation that if there had been any good faith on the Austrian side, peace must have been ensured. Austria willed the war . . . Austria appears to count on Germany; but the German Socialists declare that secret treaties do not bind the proletariat. The German proletariat say that Germany must not intervene even if Russia does. The German bourgeoisie maintain, on the contrary, that Germany must intervene with the equally logical and obvious consequences that the French bourgeoisie think France must intervene against Germany. The French proletariat think as we do.'

Adler, for Austria, frankly admitted the inability of the Austrian Socialists to check the bellicose movement in their country, which drew upon him the rebukes of the German delegates.

Jaurès declared that the French Socialists had no need to urge a pacific policy on their Government, which was already practising it.

> 'I have earned the right to say that at this moment the French Government desires peace. It is the greatest ally for peace of that admirable

English Government, which has taken the initiative in conciliation, and it is giving Russia counsels of prudence and patience.'

Much more was said in favour of peace, but nothing whatever done or attempted. A proposal was indeed made on behalf of the French trade unions for common action with the Germans, but without effect. This happened at the Belgian trade union congress on July 25, at which Jouhaux, the head of the French General Confederation, and Legien, general secretary of the German social-democratic unions, were present as guests. Jouhaux asked Legien, in the presence of Belgian and French trade union leaders:

> "What are you thinking of doing to avoid the coming war? Do you intend to make a move? We are ready on our side, to march at your call, or to march at the same time as you."

Legien was silent. It is impossible to acquit the Germans of double dealing. On 1st August there arrived in Paris an envoy from the Executive Committee of the German Socialist Party, named Müller, nominally for information with a view to mutual action, particularly in regard to the war credits. He declared positively that the German Socialists would not vote for the credits; he regarded that as out of the question. There were only two opinions among them as to their course of action; (1) to vote against the credits, (2) to abstain. He said the majority were for the former, but if the advocates of abstention prevailed, it would be to preserve unity of action with the French Socialists, which was the great object. The obvious intention was to induce the French Socialists not to support their Government in resisting attack, in the belief that the German comrades would do the same.

What happened? While this very conference was proceeding, Germany declared war on Russia, although Austria had accepted the principle of mediation. The next day (2nd August) German troops invaded Luxembourg and crossed the French frontier without declaring war; on 3rd August Germany declared war on France; on 4th August Belgium was attacked, and the same day the German Socialists voted the war credits in the Reichstag like one man. As for the proletariat, we have the description of their delirious jubilation by Dr. Poutsma, the South African Socialist, among other eye-witnesses. Once more rang out on every hurdy-gurdy and in every heart 'Deutschland über Alles,' on every hill-top blazed the sacrificial fires of patriotic enthusiasm.

So the second International went up in smoke after twenty-five years of existence. No doubt its promoters meant well in regard to war, but the more sincere they were, the more they deceived themselves by repeating phrases such as the 'solidarity of the class-conscious proletariat.' At the touch of reality the proletariat and the Socialists alike forgot all about class and were conscious only of their country. The thing was an imposing make-believe. There was never much proletariat in it, and precious little solidarity. As a British delegate once put it, they brought up the heaviest artillery loaded with apple dumplings.

It was a debating society of theorists who could never agree when they approached any practical question and who for the most part did not belong to the class they professed to represent. Sir W. Gilbert created no more whimsical piece of topsy-turvydom than the solidarity of class-conscious proletarianism exhibited by a company of lawyers, doctors, authors, journalists, professors, civil servants, teachers, capitalists and employers shouting out rival theories in a babel of tongues and striving to assert the claims of their own country.

Chapter VII

MARX AND MARXISM

I have said that the whole of the second historical phase of Socialism was dominated by Marx, in contrast to the first phase, in which no single dominant influence can be named. It is true that at the beginning of the period with which we have been dealing counter-influences within the movement strove with his, emanating from men of his own generation who had gone through the same mental mill—Lassalle on the one hand and Bakunin on the other—and it is true that towards the end of the period, these influences asserted themselves again in spirit though in different forms, Bakunin being represented by Syndicalism and Lassalle by what we may call Fabianism. But, nevertheless, the broad fact remains that Marxism was the dominant creed throughout, and so much so that even the counter influences drew something from it. There is no question that the outstanding name in Socialism, over-topping all others, is that of Marx.

This dominance is a remarkable fact, not easy of explanation. The ordinary explanation, assumed or expressed, that Marx was a great original thinker, has been found untenable, and the more it is examined the less tenable it is found to be. Whatever the cause of his ascendancy may be it does not lie in originality. That claim rests on ignorance of his predecessors. Indeed, few men, prominent in the history of Socialism, have so little title to originality; the claim is no longer made on his behalf by any well-informed student of the subject and is merely repeated to enhance his authority with the uneducated. It will be sufficient at this point to call one witness, Dr. Hammacher, of Berlin University, whose treatise entitled *Das philosophisch—ökonomische System des Marxismus* is the most exhaustive study of Marxism yet produced. Anyone who does not know it or has not made an equally close study can hardly pretend to be well-informed. Dr. Hammacher is a highly sympathetic and most conscientious critic; he goes systematically and minutely into every point in logical sequence, first expounding Marx's position with innumerable quotations from all his writings and then subjecting each to a critical scrutiny. His summary conclusion on the question of Marx's originality is that 'in hardly any point of his doctrines was he really original.' Hammacher does not lay any great stress on the lack of originality, and rather takes the line that it does not matter, but he is obliged to note the fact although his survey, full as it is, does not include the writer from whom Marx borrowed more than from anyone else, namely Sismondi.

It is possible to lay too much stress on priority and plagiarism, but Marx is a special case because it has been a regular practice to exalt his authority by giving him credit for other men's ideas and also because of his own attitude. If Communism is to extend to ideas let it be so and assign no property rights to any individual. But that was not the way of Marx or his followers. When he wanted to attack Proudhon he could cite a string of English writers in order to prove his opponent's lack of originality; but when he used the same ideas himself he put them forward as his own and said nothing about the English writers. An instance is the claim made by Engels in his attack on Dühring, which was authorised by Marx, that to Marx belonged the credit of having made the great discovery of surplus value whereby Socialism for the first time became scientific.[1] But this discovery had been made long before by others and notably by William Thompson and Sismondi, both of whom Marx had read. Marxian writers themselves have laid much stress on priority and at one time carried on a great dispute about the respective claims of Marx and Rodbertus, of which Anton Menger drily remarks that it would never have arisen if both had not refrained with equal care from confiding the sources of their views to the public.[2]

Marx was, in truth, a great plagiarist, and his immense vogue can with much more reason be attributed to that character than to an originality he did not possess. What he did was to put other men's ideas together and make a connected whole of them. Professor Masaryk's remark that he only formulated what was, so to speak, hanging in the air, does not quite fit the case. That has sometimes been done in the history of thought at the right moment with immense effect. But the ideas that

[1] Later, after Marx's death, he allowed that there had been predecessors, but the old claim was allowed to stand.

[2] *The Right to the Whole Produce of Labour*, p. 84.

Marx formulated were not hanging in the air ; they had been formulated in definite terms by predecessors and in some cases much more clearly and eloquently than by Marx himself ; they were the defined views of schools of thought. What he did was not to give form and expression to vague notions floating about in men's minds, but to take a number of quite definite thoughts already expressed, some in Germany, some in France, and some in England, and work them into a unified system as a weaver takes so many separate threads and weaves them into a piece of cloth.

To do this required extraordinary intellectual powers, and these he brought to bear. He had an exceptional equipment of academic knowledge and an exceptional capacity for reasoning things out. His was a pre-eminently systematic mind, as some one has said. That was the German in him, for the Germans are distinguished by an exceptional capacity for assimilation and methodical application, far more than by inventiveness. But there was something more in Marx, which he owed to the Jewish side of his character ; and that was an ardent temperament inclined to revolt against the whole order of Western civilisation. It is no mere coincidence that among all the Hegelian disciples of that generation Jews should have been foremost in interpreting Hegel's philosophy in the revolutionary or, at least, extreme radical sense.

Now the secret of Marx's influence seems to lie in this combination of academic accomplishment with revolutionary ardour. The one imposes on certain minds, the other appeals to certain temperaments ; and the two may very well go together.

It was Marx's superior academic knowledge that impressed Engels, who had not had the same education, and it accounts for his Boswellian devotion. Lassalle, who had the same equipment as Marx and at least as much ability, was not so impressed. It is the parade of learning in *Das Kapital* that impresses the Labour Colleges to-day, but leaves the Fabians cold. The Principal of the London Labour College once drew my attention admiringly to the sixteen pages of names quoted at the end of the English translation of Vol. I of *Das Kapital*. I had noticed them before and also—what had apparently escaped him—that the list is mere parade, because no references to their use in the book are given. The effect of academic learning is enhanced in Marx's case by the very obscurity of his style on the Lucretian principle:

> *Omnia enim stolidi magis admirantur amantque*
> *Inversis quæ sub verbis latitantia cernunt,*

which may be translated:

> For fools the more admire and praise
> When meaning's hid in twisted phrase.

But it is not to the intellectual quality of his work that Marx owes his vitality, because it has been subject to prolonged and minute scrutiny, which has gradually sapped it away. This criticism has come from Socialists as well as non-Socialists and it has been quite impersonal, as Sombart, a most friendly critic, has said:

> 'Here and there a stone was removed from the edifice of the Marxian system; a whole army of moles, hailing from the Socialist as well as from the bourgeois camp, endangered the foundations on which it stood, until at last the whole structure collapsed as silently as the Campanile in Venice.'

And yet Marx seems as much alive as ever; his is still the name to conjure with. How is this? The explanation lies in the second of the qualities mentioned above — his revolutionary ardour. The live Marx is not the *Akademiker*, but the revolutionary; not the laborious author of the longest, most involved and most inconsistent argument ever put on paper, but the composer of the Communist Manifesto, the class war formula. Whenever the revolutionary ferment rises up, the Communist Manifesto and Marx are resuscitated with it. He does not keep revolution going; it keeps him going because he gave it a good resounding battle-cry, which still comes in handy. And that is why the defence of Marx, whether it be against the charge of plagiarism or of inconsistency or of fallacy and false prediction, always ends on the same note. After all, it doesn't matter; he preached the class war.

In one way it does not matter, but in another it does, because the revolutionary agitator and the academic theorist were two sides of the same man, and because support for the former is drawn from the latter. Proletarians of all lands are still urged to unite and throw off their chains on the strength of the economic arguments evolved by Marx to justify the class war. It is, therefore, necessary to understand the doctrine, at least in its main features.

The great claim made for Marxism is that it is 'scientific' in contrast to all other forms of Socialism. What docs this precisely mean? Science, as commonly understood, is a particular kind of knowledge, more exact than other kinds. It is more exact because it deals with things and forces which can be accurately counted, weighed, measured, or otherwise gauged, and its peculiar authority, which has for about 100 years or rather more overridden all others, rests on this superior exactness. When 'science says' this, that or the other, the dictum is accepted as final, no matter what may be said to the contrary—accepted, that is to say, until science itself says something different, which very often happens, because to err is human, as someone has truly remarked, and men of science are, after all, only human. They are liable to make mistakes through faulty or incomplete observation and still more through hasty generalisation from inadequate data. That, however, is accidental; it only means that there are degrees of scientific accuracy and does not affect the essential character and function of science, which is the attainment of exact knowledge by the means indicated.

Now it is obvious that the term 'scientific' in this sense cannot be directly applied to any movement, cause, policy, action or practical effort, such as Socialism is, if it is anything more than abstract theory. That is what Sombart meant when he called scientific Socialism a 'contradiction in terms.' No action or movement can be invested with the attributes of knowledge; the two are on different planes. All that can be said of any practical effort is that it is in accordance with science or based on scientific principles or something of that kind; and this is no doubt what is meant by scientific Socialism. It is a short way of saying Socialism in accordance with science or on scientific lines.

There is no harm in this usage provided that it is understood; the same form of expression is commonly applied to other things. But the exactness of knowledge implied by the word science remains, and the validity of the claim to superiority depends upon it. Are the underlying principles of Marxism really scientific? Before answering this question it should be noted that the German word for science—*Wissenschaft*—has a much broader meaning; it includes other and less exact forms of knowledge than science proper. But it is clear from several passages that what Marx, and Engels too, had in mind in claiming a scientific character for their system was the narrower and more precise meaning of the word, which carries with it all the authority and claim to certainty of physical science.

In the passage, at the end of Volume I of *Das Kapital*, summing up his argument and foretelling the economic revolution he uses the expression 'with the inevitability of a law of Nature,' which leaves no doubt whatever on the subject. What we call a law of Nature is the expression of a general relation of cause and effect induced from the exact observation of physical phenomena. If such a law is valid—if the observations are accurate and sufficient, and the reasoning sound—then it not only explains what actually happens or has happened but enables us to predict what will happen in given conditions. This power alone gives it utility and at the same time affords a test of its validity. For instance, the laws of astronomy enable an astronomer to predict the movements of heavenly bodies and we regulate our affairs accordingly. The laws of chemistry tell us what will happen when certain conditions are present or certain things are done. If the prediction fails there is something wrong with the law; either the observations are inaccurate or the reasoning unsound, or both. Marxian Socialism, by its claim to scientific certainty, challenges the same test of experience.

What then, are the scientific laws formulated by Marx?

They are: (1) the law of social evolution in general, commonly known as the materialist conception of history (an expression used by Engels to describe the Marxian theory); (2) the laws of capitalist economy (the capitalist system), which are a particular application of (1).

The first is by far the most important, but it occupies very little space in the writings of Marx, which are mainly occupied with (2). The most complete statement of it that he has left, apart from the Communist Manifesto, occurs in the preface to his *Criticism of Political Economy* (1859) and is as follows:

> 'The industrial organisation of society brings men into certain necessary, involuntary relations —industrial relations—which correspond to a given stage of development of their powers of material production. The sum of these industria

relations forms the economic structure of society, the real basis on which a political and legal superstructure is raised and to which certain forms of consciousness correspond. The method of production for material needs determines the social, political and intellectual mode of living in general. It is not the consciousness of men that determines their existence, but the other way round; it is their social existence that determines their consciousness. At a certain stage of development the material productive forces of society come into conflict with the existing relations of production or—to express it in juristic terms—with the property relations within which they have hitherto operated. These relations are changed from development forms of the productive forces into fetters on them. Then a period of social revolution sets in. The alteration of the economic foundation causes the whole immense superstructure (the legal and political institutions that go with the corresponding forms of social consciousness) to topple over more or less slowly or quickly. In considering such changes, the material transformation of the economic conditions of production, which can be determined with *the precision of natural science*, should always be distinguished from the legal, political, religious, æsthetic or philosophic—in short, ideological—forms in which men become conscious of the conflict and fight it out. Our social order never disappears until all the productive forces of which it is capable are developed; and a new and higher system never takes its place before the material conditions necessary to its existence are bred within the frame of the old society itself. . . . The bourgeois system is the last antagonistic form of social production; but the productive forces developing within the bourgeois order themselves create at the same time the material conditions for resolving this antagonism. This social order, therefore, brings to a close the previous history of human society.'

This passage is given because it is Marx's own (except the italics), and it contains all the essential points in his law of social evolution; but it is a condensed statement, rather clumsily worded, and anything but clear. A much fuller explanation is given by Engels in his controversial essay against Dühring (1877), an able academic Socialist of the older 'Utopian' order, who had severely criticised the Marxian doctrines; but it is too long to quote. A shorter statement by Engels, written in 1883 as a preface to a new edition of the Communist Manifesto, puts the main ideas very clearly, and has a particular interest because of its connection with the Manifesto. It is as follows:

'The pervading and basic thought of the Manifesto is that in every historical epoch the prevailing mode of economic production and exchange, and the social organisation necessarily following upon it, form the basis upon which is built up and by which alone can be explained the political and intellectual history of that epoch; that consequently the whole history of mankind (since the dissolution of primitive tribal society, holding land in common ownership) has been a history of class struggles, contests between exploiting and exploited, ruling and oppressed classes; but that this struggle has nowadays reached a stage of development in which the exploited and oppressed—the proletariat—cannot attain their emancipation from the sway of the exploiting and ruling—the bourgeoisie—without at the same time and once for all emancipating society at large from all exploitation, oppression, class distinctions and class struggles.'[1]

This is, in brief, the burthen of the Communist Manifesto, which, as Sombart remarks, contains all the vital elements in the Marxian doctrine; and Engels says that the credit for it belonged exclusively to Marx. We may put it in a series of short propositions:

History is a process of social evolution in stages.

Each stage has its own material conditions, which ultimately determine the whole order of society for that stage, and its own economic system appropriate to those conditions.

The economic system or mode of production entails the division of society into classes, which are in antagonism or develop antagonism, through being in the position of dominant and dominated, or exploiting and exploited.

The passing of society from each stage to the next, which constitutes progress, is effected by means of this class antagonism, which gradually swells until it bursts the existing order, and

[1] Version issued by the Socialist Labour Party, 1900.

ushers in a new one. This happens when the material conditions are ripe for the formation of the new order.

The present class antagonism is between the bourgeoisie and the proletariat. It will be the last. When it is resolved by the break-up of the existing order and the proletariat becomes dominant instead of dominated there will be only one class and no more antagonism. Therefore, proletarians of all lands, unite to achieve this consummation!

These are the essential elements of the Marxian doctrine in a nut-shell; the rest is subsidiary. As Bernstein, one of the leading German Socialists, puts it in his *Voraussetzungen des Sozialismus* (premises or prolegomena of Socialism), 'No one will deny that the weightiest element in the foundation of Marxism is his special theory of history, which bears the name of materialist conception of history.'

It will be seen that the doctrine is not merely an assertion of the influence exercised by material conditions in determining men's character and activities, which had been put forward by many earlier writers; it is presented as a philosophy of history, the assertion of a general principle which explains the past and is a guide to the future. That is what makes it scientific, as already explained. The principle is the law of social evolution by means of an internal antagonism, which takes the form of the class war; and this is indeed the distinctive thing in Marxism. Being a natural law, it works as a necessary inevitable process.

But before going any farther, we may ask: what happens when we get to the final term and there is no more antagonism? If there is no more antagonism, there can be no more evolution, according to the theory; but why should the principle which is responsible for past evolution fail all of a sudden and cease to operate? If the answer is that with the abolition of private ownership, and the relations consequent upon it, there will no longer be any cause for class antagonism, then we may ask why primitive society, in which that state of things already existed (see the quotation from Engels above), why or how did it ever change? Either class antagonisms were engendered in spite of communal ownership, in which case they may—and with much more reason—be engendered again, or else social evolution depends on some other principle. The dilemma is obvious; there is something wrong with the theory as it stands; the beginning and the end do not agree.

Marx never attempted to prove his theory by a detailed examination of history, showing how it worked in fact. The Communist Manifesto begins with the statement: 'The history of all hitherto existing society'—primitive communism excepted in a note—'is the history of class struggles.' Then it goes on to mention in the briefest terms some classes in the Middle Ages and in ancient Rome without even suggesting how they worked, and comes at once to modern bourgeois society which is the issue of the class antagonism generated in the preceding feudal period. Bourgeois society has in turn generated a fresh antagonism, which will destroy it, as it destroyed the feudal order;

this antagonism is between bourgeoisie and proletariat. We therefore get these two class struggles, and only these two, definitely presented—as actual examples of the process—bourgeoisie v. nobility in the feudal period—proletariat v. bourgeoisie in the present. Now, historians usually place the beginning of feudalism in the tenth century, and according to Marx the bourgeois reign which succeeded it dates only from the eighteenth century. He says (1847): 'The bourgeoisie, during its rule of scarce one hundred years . . . ' We therefore get our civilisation divided into two epochs: (1) the feudal, which lasted eight hundred years before it was completely overthrown; (2) the bourgeois, which was about to be completely overthrown after one hundred years, and is still about to be overthrown after another eighty.

This reading of history is hardly satisfactory or sufficient to fill the bill; it is, indeed, exceedingly meagre and superficial. But it is all we get to sustain the class war theory; for though other classes are mentioned in other writings of Marx, their working is not shown. The extreme poverty of the evidence suggests that Marx did not arrive at his theory by a study of the facts, but started with the theory and then found, or tried to find, facts to fit it. And that is what he actually did.

The materialist conception of history is a combination of ideas derived from (1) German philosophy, and (2) French Socialism. The first provided the form, the second the content, and Marx started with the first. He began, we may remember, with the study of philosophy, and particularly the philosophy of Hegel, who formulated a general theory of evolution as a continuous process of advance through the principle of antagonism or contradiction. It was the key to all his philosophy and is called his dialectic. This is one of the commonplaces, not only of philosophy, but of Marxian literature, in which it has been explained a hundred times. Dialectic is only another term for logic, which is the process of reasoning; and it simply means that advance from one notion to another is effected by a contradiction of the first. Every notion has, in itself, its opposite or its negation—every positive implies a negative—and from this clash a new notion arises. Marx started with this formula, but whereas Hegel conceived it in the region of abstract thought, Marx applied it to material things, to the world of reality, under the influence of Fenerbach, a minor German philosopher famous for his atheistic views; and about the time that this conversion took place, 1842–44, he also became acquainted with French Socialism, which gave him the idea of the class struggle to fill his dialectical formula. The ruling class, which is the positive, implies or carries within itself its own negative, and from this clash a new ruling class and a new social order arise. The present ruling class is the bourgeoisie and its opposite is the proletariat; the latter must, by virtue of the law, inevitably overthrow the former and form a new order.

Such are the meaning and origin of the materialist conception of history, which is both the basis and the central pillar of scientific Socialism.

I have said that Marx got the idea of the two classes from French Socialists, and I will go into that a little more fully. It is worth while, because no account exists of the origin and meaning of the words 'bourgeoisie' and 'proletariat,' which play so large a part in Socialist propaganda. They are both French terms, which have no proper equivalent in other languages, and are therefore generally transferred as they stand. Marx himself used the word 'bourgeoisie,' and when he used a German equivalent for 'bourgeois'—'*bürgerlich*'—he put it, before it became common, in inverted commas, to show that it had a technical meaning. It is, in truth, an artificial term, which explains why it had no equivalent in ordinary usage in English and German, although the root is the same in all three languages; namely *bourg* in French, *burg* in German, and 'burgh' or 'borough' in English, meaning simply 'town.' Properly 'bourgeois,' as a substantive, means a townsman or citizen, and the equivalents are *bürger* and 'burgher,' or 'burgess,' which are honourable terms.

But in France the word acquired a peculiar significance, and became a term of contempt mainly through the comedies of Molière in the seventeenth century. He held up the townsman to ridicule, in contrast to the nobleman or gentleman, not because of his social standing, but because of his manners and ignorance; he represented a type of character rather than an economic class, though the two were generally associated. Hence the use of the word as an epithet. And this meaning still clung to it when the Revolution destroyed the privileges of nobility and clergy, and put power into the hands of tradesmen, who were regarded as common, vulgar fellows. They themselves avoided the term 'bourgeois' for that reason, and used 'citizen' (*citoyen*).

'Proletariat' was still more artificial. It is a Latin word that came up in the Revolution, when the fashion was to introduce Latin words and names. It was used by Robespierre in the sitting of the National Convention of June 17th, 1793, when he opposed a proposal to exempt the poor from all taxation; he said that this would create a class of proletarians or helots. He was then using the word in its proper sense. It was a term of contempt applied in ancient Rome to the lowest class of citizens who lived on the State and did nothing for it except produce children (*proles*). But as used by Socialists it came to mean almost exactly the opposite, as shown in the quotation from Sismondi in Chapter I, p. 8. The new proletary was still the lowest class, but instead of its living on the rest of the community, as in ancient Rome, the community was regarded as living upon it, 'on that share of the remuneration of its labour which is deducted from it'—otherwise the 'surplus value of labour.'

A precise meaning was first given to the two words and the class division formulated by Pierre Leroux and Jean Reynaud in 1832, in an article written on the occasion of a riot which took place at the funeral of General Lamarque. This is what they wrote:

> 'I say that the people are composed of two classes, distinct by condition and by interest.'

Compare this in passing with the Communist Manifesto written fifteen years later:

'Society is more and more splitting up into two great hostile camps, into two great classes directly facing each other—bourgeoisie and proletariat.'

The Frenchmen, who were Saint-Simonian Socialists, continue:

'I call proletarians the men who produce all the wealth of the nation, but who possess only the daily wage of their labour and whose labour depends on causes outside themselves; who draw each day but a small portion of the fruit of their toil and are constantly reduced by competition; for whom every to-morrow depends on no more stable hope than the uncertain and irregular movement of industry; and who see no security for their old age but a hospital bed or premature death.[1]

One of the most surprising claims made on behalf of Marx is the intense sympathy with the poor revealed in his writings. Can any passage be quoted from him so simple, so concise, and yet so eloquent, as the foregoing? Yet it can be matched by many from other writers of the pre-Marxian period. It would, indeed, be difficult to find one not superior in this respect to Marx, who professedly abjured the moral appeal. What his eulogists have mistaken for sympathy with the poor is hatred of the

[1] Leroux, *Œuvres* I, p. 358.

rich, which runs through all his writings. The tirade against the bourgeoisie, which occupies so much space in the Communist Manifesto, is a hymn of hate. There is a snarl in every page.

To return to our French authors, they proceed to enumerate the proletarians—town and country labourers—and they conclude 'in short, twenty-two millions of persons uneducated, neglected, wretched, reduced to sustain life on twelve farthings a day.' They evidently had in mind the rising of the Lyons weavers in the previous year, already described in Chapter II, pp. 39-40. Then they go on to define the bourgeoisie as the men to whose fortune that of the proletariat is subject and bound, who possess capital and live on the annual return yielded by it, who hold industry in their pay and raise or lower it according to their sales . . . in short *the proprietors*, from the richest to the poorest ; the manufacturers and feudal lords of industry.[1]

This view of society, which gave precision to previous vague ideas, just suited Marx's interpretation of history and also his revolutionary leanings, developed about the same time. He was to some extent acquainted with French Socialism before he went to Paris in 1843. It had been made generally known in Germany by the account of Lorenz Von Stein published in 1842 and by a scientific congress held at Strasbourg the same year, at which some French Socialists, including Leroux, were present ; but it was no doubt mainly in Paris that Marx picked up the French ideas which he worked into

[1] Leroux, *Œuvres* I, pp. 358–60.

his own system, and among others the bourgeoisie-proletariat formula. But it is to be noted that the French thinkers hit at once on ownership as the crucial distinction, whereas Marx only arrived at it in the last volume of *Das Kapital*, where he says that ' the relation of the owners to the immediate producers (labourers) is the inmost secret, the hidden basis of the whole social structure.' Now ownership is in itself a legal, not an economic, condition; but previously in the passage quoted above he had made economic conditions the basis of the legal structure; here the position is reversed. Which really comes first?

This, however, is merely one of the many ambiguities or inconsistencies to be found in the Marxian argument. A more important difference between his reading of the class division and the original is that the latter was much less absolute; it did not represent society as completely split in two. Leroux recognised that there were intermediate and mixed classes—greys as well as blacks and whites. Still less did he regard the classes as separated by an absolute antagonism; he did not put them in hostile camps, as Marx did. On the contrary he maintained that though their views and interests were separate they were not contradictory and that ' the progress that had become necessary to preserve society could be achieved otherwise than by civil war.' He urged co-operation in the exercise of power and regulation by common accord, and deprecated the class war. The appeal to class war which is still to-day the net outcome of all Marx's theories, was Marx's own, and he is entitled to the credit of having preached the most poisonous doctrine ever poured into the ears of men—a doctrine involving the deliberate cultivation of hatred and universal strife. Just as he gave Hegel's dialectic a materialistic turn so he gave Leroux's class division a revolutionary twist.

Before leaving the materialist conception of history I will briefly refer to the opinion of the most eminent thinker who has studied it. I mean Benedetto Croce, the distinguished Italian philosopher. He recognises the value of Marx's insistence on the part played by economic conditions in history, previously neglected, but holds that his theory is not and cannot be a new philosophy of history; it is only a 'canon of historical interpretation'—that is, a rule or generalisation which explains some things. Of the class war theory he says that 'history is a class-war (1) when there are classes; (2) when they have antagonistic interests; (3) when they are aware of this antagonism; which would give us, in the main, the somewhat humorous equivalence that history is a class war only when it is a class war.'[1] He points out that classes do not always have antagonistic interests and are very often unconscious of them, of which Socialists supply a proof by their efforts to arouse this consciousness. That is undeniable. Class-consciousness, which they have been busily arousing for the last sixty years, is only a euphemism for strife. Their efforts have been directed to exciting animosity where it did not exist, with the highest motives of course.

To pass on to the laws of capitalist economy, which form the second part of scientific Socialism

[1] Benedetto Croce: *Historical Materialism*, p. 85.

as stated above, I said that they were an application of the general law of evolution we have been discussing; by which I meant that they explain the operation of that law by revealing the processes of bourgeois economy, which must lead to its overthrow. They furnish a detailed proof of the soundness of the conclusion already formulated and justify the class war. That, at least, is the intention; and here again we see Marx's method of reasoning. He started with a philosophical formula, went on to fit into it first the historical facts, and then backed this up with economic laws in keeping. So we get a connected whole, a complete system.

The economic part was no more original than the philosophic and historical. The leading ideas were derived from Sismondi and from English writers; what Marx did was to elaborate them and adapt them to his main thesis. When Engels claimed for Marx the epoch-making discovery of surplus value, he probably did so in ignorance, for he never studied economic literature as Marx did. But there is no longer any excuse for this error and for other claims equally unfounded.

The economic theories of Marx have attracted far more attention than the rest of his system, probably because they form a contribution—a disturbing contribution—to the general theory of economics. They are often presented to students as a complete system in themselves—and the only true one; but they do not pretend to be a general theory of economics. In the preface to the first edition of *Das Kapital* Marx says that 'What I have to investigate in this work is the Capitalist mode of production and the relations entailed by it': and the opening sentence limits the inquiry to wealth as it appears in Capitalist societies, namely as a huge collection of market wares, the nature, origin and behaviour of which he proceeds to analyse. It is a limited inquiry quite obviously intended to serve a particular purpose; but it necessarily involved general economic questions in a way calculated to arouse controversy in that exceedingly controversial field. And it has done so. An enormous controversial literature has grown up on Marxian economics. Nothing in Socialism has been so much discussed both by way of attack and defence. It is therefore the less necessary to go into it here at length, though it is too important to be omitted altogether.

What Marx had to prove was that the Capitalist method of production—now called Capitalism—contains within itself the seeds of its own destruction, according to the Hegelian law of advance by affirmation—negation—negation of negation. As he puts it himself:

> 'The Capitalist mode of appropriation proceeding from the Capitalist mode of production—and hence Capitalist private property—is the first negation of individual private property based on the owner's own labour. But Capitalist production begets its own negation with the inevitability of a law of Nature. It is the negation of negation.'[1]

The basis of his argument is the famous labour theory of value, to which reference has already been

[1] *Das Kapital*, Vol. I, p. 691, Kautsky's edition.

made in Chapter I. It was formulated, as I have already said, by a series of English writers ending with Ricardo,[1] whose treatise on political economy opens with the statement, 'The value of a commodity or the quantity of any other commodity for which it will exchange, depends on the relative quantity of labour which is necessary for its production.' He then quotes Adam Smith:[2] 'The real price of everything, what everything really costs to the man who wants to acquire it, is the toil and trouble of acquiring it. Labour was the first price—the original purchase money that was paid for all things.' Before Adam Smith, John Locke, the English philosopher (1632–1704) had said the same thing in his treatises on Government (1690); and before him again Thomas Hobbes (1588–1679) had defined wealth or plenty as 'those commodities that God either freely giveth or *for labour selleth* to mankind.' Between the two last-named came Sir W. Petty (1623–1687), to whom Marx was particularly indebted for the idea of simple labour as distinguished from technical. Petty, by the way, repeatedly uses the word 'hands' for workmen. Still earlier, the real father of political economy and inventor of the term, Antoine de

[1] David Ricardo (1772–1823); Anglo-Dutch—Jewish family of Portuguese extraction; stockbroker and economist; published *Principles of Political Economy* in 1817; entered Parliament in 1819; was the last of the 'classical' economists according to Marx.

[2] Adam Smith (1723–1790); Professor of Logic and (later) of Moral Philosophy in the University of Glasgow; published the *Wealth of Nations* in 1776; was the greatest of the classical economists—the only ones whom Marx treated with respect, presumably because he got the basis of his argument from them. The later ones he called 'vulgar,' which does not mean vulgar in the English sense, but 'popular.' So Huxley and Häckel might be called vulgar evolutionists.

Montchrétien, had said in his *Traicté de L'Oeconomie Politique* (1615) that 'wealth comes from labour.'

The idea had therefore a long pedigree and was quite familiar when Marx came upon the scene. More than that, as I have shown in Chapters I and II, the natural inference had been drawn that labour—in the narrow sense of manual labour—was defrauded, because it created all value but received in wages only a small portion of the value created by itself. I have mentioned Sismondi and Thompson in this connection as the two most important writers falling within the period and under review; but the same observation had previously been made in 1805 by Charles Hall, who was not an economist but a doctor, like Quesnay the founder of the school of Physiocrats, and like him deeply stirred by the poverty he witnessed, side by side with great wealth. Marx may not have read Hall, but he had certainly read both Sismondi and Thompson. The latter Anton Menger records as 'the most eminent founder of scientific Socialism,' and says:

> 'Leaving out of account the mathematical formulæ by which Marx rather obscures than elucidates his argument, the whole theory of surplus value, its conception, its name and the estimates of its amounts are borrowed in all essentials from Thompson's writings. Only Marx, in accordance with the aim of his work, pays special attention to the one form of unearned income (interest on capital) and fails to give either that jural criticism of private property in

instruments of production and useful commodities, which is the necessary supplement of the theory of surplus value, or a rigorous exposition of the right to the whole produce of labour. In all these respects Marx is far inferior to Thompson, so that the work of the latter may be regarded as the foundation-stone of Socialism.'[1]

I have referred to Sismondi on surplus value in Chapter I and will now quote one passage of his, together with one from Marx for the purpose of comparison. After dealing with agriculture, Sismondi goes on:

'At the same time other capitalists undertake the direction of industry; they secure wages to workmen, rent to the proprietors of mills and machines, interest to other capitalists, who are content with lending their capital without wishing to give themselves any trouble; they pay taxes to government; they keep a profit for themselves; they are thus the distributors of an annual income to four or five classes of persons; but this income, whether obtained in the country or in towns, is never anything but the surplus of the value of what labour has produced above the advances made to produce it.'[2]

Thus Marx:

'Rent, interest and industrial profit are only different names for different parts of the surplus

[1] Menger: *The Right to the Whole Produce of Labour*, p. 101.
[2] *Revue Mensuelle d'Economie Politique*, 1835.

value of the commodity, or the unpaid labour enclosed in it, and they are equally derived from this source, and from this source alone.'[1]

So much for the discovery of surplus value. But Sismondi supplied Marx with far more than that. His exposition of the inevitable effects of competition in lowering the status of labour, the creation of proletarians, the crushing of small capitalists and businesses by large ones, the concentration of capital, the recurrence of 'crises' (trade depressions), under-consumption through low wages, the technical developments of industry and their unfavourable effects, the divorce of ownership and work, the reduction of workmen to machines without intelligence or interest in their work, the abyss between opulence and indigence—all these put forward by Sismondi are the very marrow of the Marxian argument. But there is a great difference. Sismondi described what existed at the time, but he did not assume that those conditions and tendencies would go on progressively getting worse and worse, until the whole order broke down and an economic revolution took place. Marx did assume this; it was essential to his case. He sums it up in a passage as 'the historical tendency of capitalist accumulation' at the end of Chapter XXIV of *Das Kapital* (Kautsky's edition). The new economic transformation that is coming, he says, in consequence of capitalist development, is the expropriation of the capitalist employing many workmen.

[1] *Value, Price and Profit*, written in 1865, published posthumously.

'This expropriation fulfils itself through the play of the immanent laws of capitalist production itself, through the centralisation of capital. One capitalist always strikes many dead. Hand in hand with this centralisation or expropriation of many capitalists by few there develops the co-operative form of the labour process on an ever ascending scale, the purposeful technical application of science, the systematic exploitation of the earth, the transformation of the instruments of labour into instruments usable only in common, the economising of all means of production by their use as means of combined social labour, the drawing of all peoples into the net of the world market and therewith the international character of the capitalist régime. With the constantly diminishing number of capitalist magnates, who usurp and monopolise all the benefits of this transformation process, grows the mass of misery, oppression, servitude, degradation, exploitation; but also the revolt of the working class, constantly growing in number and schooled, united and organised by the mechanism of the capitalist method of production. The monopoly of capital becomes a fetter on the mode of production, which has flourished with and under it. The centralisation of the means of production and the socialisation of labour reach a point at which they become incompatible with the capitalist shell enclosing them. It is burst asunder. The knell of capitalist private property sounds. The expropriators are expropriated.'

This course of events, he goes on to explain, is

in conformity with the law of historical evolution, as already indicated, and inevitable, like a process of Nature. The outcome will be co-operation and common ownership of the land and means of production. The prediction, which was repeated with a few more details, but in almost identical terms, in the Erfurt Programme,[1] rests on the progressive development of the conditions described by Sismondi, and since it is endowed with the certainty proper to a scientific law it is subject to the same test of experience. Other forms of Socialism being efforts or aspirations towards an ideal, are not disposed of by failure; they can try again. But for a scientific law there is no escape; it must answer to the test or be condemned. Has scientific Socialism answered to it?

Nobody any longer pretends that the facts fully correspond with Marx's forecast. What Marxians now say is that he was right up to a point, but did not foresee certain developments that have taken place since. That is admitted; but, they contend, this makes no difference. On the whole, in spite of some miscalculations, his theory is perfectly sound. That will not do. A scientific law that is only partly correct is worse than useless. A bridge, a dam, an engine, a ship, built according to such a law is a danger; similarly with a chemical reaction, a mathematical calculation or an astronomical observation. Any flaw destroys the certainty which is the peculiar property and the criterion of a scientific law—a certainty repeatedly claimed by Marx and Engels for his theory.

[1] See page 57.

Without insisting, however, on this strict interpretation of 'scientific,' let us examine the contention that, on the whole, Marx was right, and that economic development has been and is proceeding in the direction he indicated. The features of industrial and commercial evolution he enumerates may be allowed; but what of the 'concentration of capital' and 'the constantly diminishing number of capitalist magnates' who alone benefit by these changes? And what of the constantly growing mass of misery, oppression, etc., which is the other side of the concentration of capital? This is the point; for if the industrial development has not produced those effects, then it is not moving in the direction foretold by Marx. And it has not produced them.

The concentration of capital has not gone on progressively, the number of magnates has not constantly diminished, the large capitalist has not eliminated the small one. On the contrary, there has been a great and growing diffusion of capital, the number of magnates has increased,[1] and the small concern has not only survived but multiplied alike in agriculture, commerce and industry. The diffusion of capital has been effected through joint stock companies, savings banks, provident societies, building societies, and numerous other agencies which vary in different countries. In Lancashire, for instance, ninety per cent. of the spinning mill workers have loan or share capital, or both, in the mills. In France, the banks gather up every little

[1] Marx recognised the increased number of capitalists in Vol. III of *Das Kapital*. It is one of the numerous contradictions in that work.

sum saved by the humblest people—maid-servants, day labourers, factory workers, clerks, small officials, shop assistants, peasants—and invest it. The noble repudiation of the claims of Russian bondholders by the Moscow Government, applauded by Socialists, hit no one so hard as these small people —the French proletariat. The channels of saving and investment are continually multiplying and expanding. So far from the small and medium capitalists being driven down to the ranks of the proletariat, the modern movement is for the proletariat to become small and medium capitalists.

The multiplication of income taxpayers up to millionairedom, in contradiction to Marx's concentration theory, cannot be denied; but Socialists constantly refer to the formation of capitalist combines, trusts, syndicates, kartells, or whatever they may be called, as demonstrating the correctness of the theory. It does not; this movement represents concentration of management, not of capital. In many cases, it is accompanied by a fresh diffusion of capital on a large scale and an increased number of shareholders. As for the disappearance of the small concern eaten up by the large one, it is completely disproved by a mass of statistics, of which I can only find space for a few. The number of small (1–5 persons) and middle-sized (6–50 persons) concerns in Germany, the most rapidly developing State in the period covered by the censuses, was as follows:

	1882	1895	1907
Small ...	2,882,768	2,934,723	3,124,198
Middle ..	112,715	191,301	267,410

There are two movements going on together: (1) Increase in the size of concerns; (2) Continuous renewal of small concerns, which have increased, not diminished, in number. In the American statistics we get another category in the single-handed independent concern. These increased in the United States between 1909 and 1914 from 27,712 to 32,856, and the number of persons employed in small (1–5) concerns from 136,289 to 140,971. These were the only two classes which increased their percentages of the total number. What really happens, both in the industrial and the commercial world, is that while large concerns do eat up some small ones they at the same time breed others. Enterprising workmen set up for themselves, (1) to execute repairs, and make (2) accessories; (3) parts; and enterprising shop-assistants set up for themselves to sell particular classes of goods, which they thoroughly understand, in the very neighbourhood of the large stores, where customers congregate. The process may be observed going on in large towns; I have observed it for many years. Also the industrial development has itself revived the home-worker and the 'little master' by the supply of electrical power, as in Germany and France. In agriculture the case is still stronger; the number of small holdings has everywhere increased at the expense of the large.

And if the facts disprove that side of the prediction, the other, which postulates increasing misery, has been even more completely falsified. Marx himself emphasised[1] the 'moral and physical

[1] *Das Kapital*, Vol. I, pp. 241–2.

regeneration' of the Lancashire people through the Act of 1847, which was the first of a long series of factory laws. To maintain, as is still sometimes done, that the state of the working classes is no better than it used to be is to contend that not only industrial and public health legislation but also municipal services, trade unions and co-operative societies have done nothing to improve conditions. But even the hardiest agitator does not affirm that conditions are worse, and every elderly workman knows that they have vastly improved. Speaking at an I.L.P. Conference on April 12, 1924, Robert Smillie said that working conditions were much better to-day than they were formerly.

The theory of increasing misery is, indeed, so untenable that it has long been formally abandoned and replaced by the singular theory of relative misery. What is relative misery? The meaning of 'misery' has never been defined, but it is wider than poverty. So, too, with the corresponding German terms *Elend* and *Armuth*. *Elend* generally conveys a sense of mental rather than bodily distress, and so does misery; the very word miser is applied to a pecuniarily rich, not a poor man. The theory of relative misery, put forward in 1901 by Kautsky and Bebel to make the Marxian doctrine square with the facts, implies that no matter how much better off you may be, you are more miserable than before if some one else is still better off. What a view of human nature!

But the pretence that Marx did not mean absolute misery will not do. The expression in the Communist Manifesto is, 'The modern labourer sinks deeper and deeper below the conditions of his own class.' Nor is it true that he and Engels withdrew this in the preface to the edition of 1872. They said that the programme at the end of Part II, dealing with revolutionary measures, and the remarks about Communists and other parties, were antiquated; but they did not withdraw the increasing misery, which was the lynch pin of the class war chariot. Nor did Marx describe it as merely a tendency, which might be counteracted by other tendencies; it was inevitable by the immanent laws of Capitalism. It is true that he also made the reference to the effects of the English Factory Act of 1847 quoted above; but that does not save the theory. It is only one of the numerous inconsistencies, which caused Bernstein to say that 'one can prove anything out of Marx and Engels.'

The only version of the theory at all in keeping with the facts is that of relative poverty. It may be contended that to-day the very rich are farther than ever removed from the poor. But that holds good only of the command of money, not of real wealth. Beyond a certain point the accumulation of money is of no practical use, as wise men have pointed out in every age; it can be converted into no more of the necessaries, comforts, conveniences and even superfluous enjoyments of life, because the owners' capacity for absorption is exhausted, and more money is nothing but a burden. From this point onwards the differentiation between rich and poor becomes purely arithmetical, and that is the case to-day with extreme riches.

In all the things that matter there has been an increasing approximation, not separation, of class conditions. There has been a levelling up at one end and a levelling down at the other. It stares one in the face in visible matters of the first importance—houses, clothes and locomotion. Perhaps the first affords the most striking object lesson. No one to-day dreams of building a Blenheim, a Chatsworth or a Castle Howard; and no one builds such cottages for labourers as represented the other end of the scale when the palaces were reared. As for clothes, it is no longer possible, as it used to be, to distinguish classes by clothes, masculine or feminine. And locomotion. In the happy days before the arrival of modern capitalism only the rich could travel at all; everyone else was limited to walking. Now all use the same conveyances; the only appreciable difference between first and third class on the railways is the relative amount of space, and if capitalists dash about by road in their own cars the proletariat do the same in charabancs. To-day the poorest emigrants cross the Atlantic with all the speed and security commanded by the rich, whose margin of superiority, ease and luxury is constantly diminishing. He that has eyes to see let him see!

The theory of relative misery is no more tenable than the other, and the whole Marxian argument, tested by experience, crumbles away. The course of social development has not only diverged in certain details from the Marxian forecast, as Marxians admit; it has broadly proceeded in the opposite direction. There must therefore be something wrong with his reasoning. In truth it abounds in fallacies, which have been exposed by a whole stream of critics, more often dispassionate or benevolent than hostile—Sombart's ' army of moles ' previously mentioned. It has been done so often and so fully and has elicited such a feeble reply, containing little but a dogged repetition of the discredited formulas or counter-criticism of ' orthodox ' economics, that one might be excused from going over the same ground again. The weakness of the marginal utility theory of value, which must be fully admitted by any candid critic, does not make Marx's labour theory strong, as the Labour College economists seem to suppose. Partly because of this superabundance of criticism and partly because the aim of this book is rather historical and explanatory than critical, as I have said in the preface, I have approached the question on the other side. But having by an examination of the facts, necessarily brief, but capable of indefinite extension, reached the conclusion that there must be fallacies in the argument, which has been so signally contradicted by experience, I ought perhaps to indicate their nature.

The primary reason for Marx's failure to make theory correspond with fact was that he set out to prove a foregone conclusion—a conclusion already stated in the Communist Manifesto when he was under the revolutionary spell and before he had made any serious study of economics at all. His theme was the exploitation of labour, and his analysis of modern capitalist economy was directed to revealing the mechanism or process of exploitation. Hence his adoption of the labour theory of value in its narrowest form as the starting-point of his investigation. In order to make labour the sole source (apart from Nature), and the measure of value puts him wrong at the outset, he begins by omitting all goods or wares, whose market value is not affected by labour but is affected by their utility or capacity to satisfy some want and by their scarcity—such as objects of art, old books, furniture, wine, etc.

Then he eliminates the factor of utility or usefulness altogether. He argues that goods which exchange for one another in the market are equal in value —so much wheat for so much blacking or silk or gold, or whatever it may be. This means that they must have something in common to them all and present in equal quantity in each. What is it? It cannot be their particular properties or qualities because these 'come into consideration only in so far as they make the things useful, that is, make use values of them. But on the other hand the exchange value of the goods obviously disregards their utility.[1] Within the exchange relation of the goods—or for exchange purposes—one use value is just as good as another provided that it is present in the right proportion. . . . As use values the goods are before everything of different qualities; as exchange values they can be only different quantities and consequently contain not an atom of use value.'

If, then, he goes on, we disregard the use value of the article, they have only one property left, that of being the products of labour. But, he continues, if we take out the use value we must also take out the material properties which confer

[1] This sentence, which begs the whole question, and is here literally translated from the original, is rendered by a rather obscure paraphrase in the current English version.

use value, and with these again the different kinds of labour embodied in them; the latter must be all 'reduced to equal human labour, abstract, simple, human labour.' This constitutes their value. It follows that use values or goods have value only because abstract human labour is realised or materialised in them. And the amount of value is measured by the quantity of the value-creating substance, labour, embodied in them. Q.E.D.

If one could suspect Marx of joking, which is impossible—such elephantine playfulness as calling the capitalist 'Mr. Moneybags' is the translator's, not Marx's, little joke—one must suppose that he penned that argument with his tongue in his cheek; for he understood logic very well, and a prettier specimen of the fallacy, *petitio principii*, or 'begging the question,' would be difficult to find. It consists in assuming the conclusion you are going to prove. Marx wants to prove that labour is the sole source and the measure of value and he does it by taking out everything else. He says that because the utilities in different articles are all different, they have for exchange purposes no utility at all. Then why do they exchange? You might just as well turn it round the other way and say that because the labour embodied in different articles is different, one kind is as good as another for exchange purposes, and therefore there is none at all in them. But that would not suit his argument; so instead of treating the difficulty of different kinds of labour as he has treated the different utilities that go with them, he reduces them all to simple abstract labour. Obviously the different utilities can be treated in the same way and reduced to simple abstract utility. He is obliged to admit a little lower down that use value is there after all: 'Nothing can be a value (that is, exchange value) without being an object of utility (that is, having use value).' Of course it cannot, for if an article is of no use nobody wants it or will give anything for it. Utility is, in fact, a much more constant factor in exchange value than labour. You may have exchange value without labour—as in the class of goods referred to above—and you may have labour that confers no exchange value, as in those useless articles just mentioned. Marx himself says so: 'If a thing is useless, so too is the labour embodied in it; it does not count as labour and confers no value.'

The last touch, that labour does not count as labour unless it confers utility—which has previously been eliminated when it did not suit the argument—is really grotesque, if not intended to be ironical. It is possible to prove anything if awkward facts which do not accord with the conclusion can be disposed of by saying that they 'do not count.' Nothing counts in the Marxian system of economics unless it fits the desired conclusion. Wealth that does not consist of market goods does not count as wealth; value that is not created by labour does not count as value, and labour that does not create value does not count as labour. It is not surprising that one critic speaks of Marx's 'hocus-pocus' and his most brilliant living defender credits him with 'playful mystification.' Playful mystification indeed! Such a description of the premisses to the great argument on which he spent sixteen laborious years is more damaging than any direct condemnation.

And this is only the beginning. The logical difficulties and contradictions in which Marx entangles himself from the outset increase as he goes on. But I have devoted too much space to him already and can only refer briefly to one or two further developments.

We have got to this point—that goods which exchange for one another in the market are of equivalent value, and that this is measured by the quantity of abstract labour required to produce them under average conditions at the time, otherwise 'socially necessary' labour. It follows that they are all exchanged—bought and sold—at their real value. Where, then, does the capitalist's profit—we are dealing with capitalist production—come from? If all the factors employed in production, including labour, are bought at their real value, and the product is sold at its real value, the two must exactly coincide and there can be no profit. The originators of the theory of surplus value held, as I have shown, that profit was secured by deducting so much from the proper remuneration of labour, that is by paying workmen less than their true value. But in that case the law of equivalent values, according to which labour must be bought like other things at its real value, would be violated. Here is a dilemma.

Marx solved the problem by a discovery, which Engels extols as one of his greatest achievements; namely that what the capitalist buys and the labourer sells is not labour, but labour power, which alone among commodities has the remarkable property of creating more value than it possesses itself. In consequence of this property it is able to create surplus value for the capitalist, though he buys it at its real value, which is the cost of its production or re-production, that is the maintenance of the labourer and his family. So the law of equivalent values is preserved and yet profit accounted for. But of course the labourer is exploited in the process. The capitalist buys his labour power for a day of so many hours, and pays its real value in the sense explained. But this value is earned by the labourer in less than the day's work—say in six hours out of twelve; value created in the remaining six hours goes to the capitalist, who thus gets his profit out of that part of the day's work for which he pays nothing. So the exploiting is done, but concealed under the day's pay, which takes no account of paid and unpaid hours.

It is not surprising that this argument, which sounds very convincing, should be popular with Labour Socialists; but it is rather surprising that other people should accept it so easily as they often do. In the first place the great discovery of labour power for labour is a great mare's nest. Labour power is just what the capitalist cannot buy because it is inseparable from the labourer's person, as Engels recognised in order to prove something else. The labourer not only brings it with him and takes it home again, but he also applies it himself and can vary the amount at pleasure. Now the essence of buying and selling is that the thing bought passes completely out of the possession of the seller into that of the buyer, who can do what he pleases with it. But this is obviously not the case with labour power. Marx assumes that it is, that the capitalist gets the whole of it and can do what he pleases with it independently of the will of its real owner. He says the labour power is just as much his as the oil he buys. He evidently had never heard of 'ca'-canny,' which is likely enough, as he had no first-hand knowledge of industry. He never entered one of those factories of which he wrote so much and knew so little. He seems to have got what he knew mainly from Engels, which accounts for the excessive prominence of cotton spinning in his exposition; and in that industry piece work and payment by results prevail.

If the capitalist can be said to buy anything it is the use of labour power for a given time; but 'the use of labour power,' says Marx, 'is labour itself.'[1] So the great distinction disappears. But even the use of it is not at the disposal of the capitalist, like the use of a machine; the labourer's will remains and, as we know very well from experience, if he is dissatisfied and does not choose to exert himself, the employer does not get what he has bought. In truth the conception of labour or labour power as a 'commodity' like any other is fundamentally false and the cause of endless trouble. The real relation is between human beings.

However, apart from this, the Marxian theory is clearly fallacious. How is it that the labourer is able to earn his value or cost of production or living (it is all one) in half a day? Only because of the means of production provided. According to Marx, these count for nothing in the creation

[1] *Das Kapital*, I, p. 133.

of value, yet he himself lays great stress on the enormous increase of productivity effected by technical developments, when he wants to prove that the capitalist gets all the benefit and that labour is more and more exploited. If living labour alone creates value, why should improved tools and processes have such an effect? Why is the same labour able to produce so much more? Again, Marx maintains that the machine always loses in value as much as it yields in the product; it merely replaces its own cost. Then why put in any machines? If, as he says, the capitalist cares for nothing but surplus value or profit, and labour power alone creates this, then why does the capitalist who, according to Marx, understands his business very well, why does he waste so much of his beloved profits on machinery which produces no surplus value? Why does he always seek to replace labour, which makes profit for him, by machinery which does not? The reply that machines make labour more intense is contrary to the facts.

The same contradiction crops up in another form, when he proceeds a little farther in his analysis and divides capital into constant and variable. Constant represents machinery and variable represents labour. Consequently, surplus value or profit should vary with the proportion in which these stand to each other; the more variable capital employed in an industry relative to the constant, the greater the profit, and the other way round. But in practice it is not so, as Marx himself admits. He states the law thus: 'The masses of value and surplus value produced by different capitals are, *cæteris paribus*, directly proportionate to the size of the variable part of such capitals, that is of the part converted into living labour power.'[1] And then goes on immediately: 'This law plainly contradicts all experience based on appearances,' with examples thereof. But no explanation is attempted, though some of the usual gibes are thrown at other economists for not explaining a contradiction they had not formulated. He evidently had not then thought out the explanation himself. Nor did he ever succeed in reconciling fact and theory, for when the promised explanation occurred in Vol. III it threw over the theory, and admitted the identity of appearance and fact. Profits do not vary according to the composition of the capital employed, but are evened out by competition. Consequently, goods are not sold at their value, but at an average rate of profit, which is no longer surplus value but becomes part of the cost of production.

This contradiction has been more discussed than any other point in the Marxian theory, and many futile attempts have been made to explain it away. The most unfortunate of all is that of Engels, who said that the law of value did hold good before the fifteenth century, that is in the pre-capitalist period! That is giving Marxism away with a vengeance; for the whole point of the great economic analysis is that it is an investigation of modern capitalism, which differs from all previous systems. If the law of value holds good of them, but not of capitalism, it has no relevance to the inquiry at all, and the whole thing falls to pieces. Nothing could show more clearly the hopeless muddle into

[1] *Das Kapital*, Vol. I, p. 255.

which Marx had worked himself in trying to prove his foregone conclusion than the plight of his faithful disciple and interpreter, thus driven to abandon the position reached with so much toil and pains.

Nor was this the only case of retreat. It was the fate of poor Engels to be compelled to water down other pronouncements essential to the logical structure they had built together. The most important is the materialist conception of history, according to which economic conditions determine all other human activities and institutions, so that 'all social and political changes issue not from men's brains, but from changes in the modes of production and exchange'; whence the class war. He likened this law of social evolution, for which he gave Marx the whole credit, to the physical law of the conservation of energy, but did not explain where the changes in production and exchange came from, if they did not come out of men's brains. However, near the end of his life he greatly modified the law and admitted that political, juridical, philosophic theories and religious views influenced the course of historical struggles, and in many cases determined their form. He still clung to the economic basis, but allowed that the various intellectual activities re-acted on it.[1]

As an economist Marx suffered from two weaknesses, apart from the initial handicap of having the ready-made thesis of exploitation to sustain. He did not recognise the psychological or subjective element and the true part played by utility in determining value; and he failed to appreciate the function of the enterpriser in initiating and

[1] Letters of 1890, 1895.

conducting an industrial concern. In Vol. I of *Das Kapital* he makes only a few perfunctory references to the element of supervision, as a thing of small account though necessary ; in Vol. III this slighting attitude is somewhat amended. He discusses the distinction between interest on capital and enterprisers' profit, and says that ' the exploitation of productive labour costs effort,' and that ' the labour of exploitation is just as much labour as the labour that is exploited.' But to him it is still only exploitation. He evidently had no conception of the real part played by what Fourier called ' talent ' and later economists ' ability ' in conducting industry. It is far more than ' management ' or ' supervision,' which was all that Marx could see. To him all the material factors in production are ready made ; he takes them for granted. True, the capitalist has to buy them, but he assumes that anybody who has the money can do that. Marx ignores, probably because he knew nothing about them, the multifarious functions of organisation and co-ordination, the planning of the whole thing, the position and lay-out of the works, the selection and procuring of tools and engines, the designing of the product, the arrangement of processes, the selection and purchase of raw materials, the disposal of the product.

If Marx had understood these operations and the knowledge, judgment and effort required to make them successful it might have occurred to him that the surplus value produced over and above the combined cost of the means of production was created by the combination, and that the all important thing was the right combination, not any mysterious property in labour power, which produces no surplus with a wrong combination and may be changed over and over again without making any difference with a right one. An illustration used more than once by Marx will bring out the omission in his view of the productive factors. He likens an industrial concern to an orchestra, in which the directing authority—required, he admits, by all combined labour on a large scale—is the conductor. In capitalist industry the place of the conductor is taken by Capital, whose function it is to direct, superintend and adjust. He forgot that in the orchestra there is someone behind the conductor and of far more importance—namely, the composer. And in industry, too, there is a composer, on whom far more depends than on all the other factors. An orchestra may, it is true, go on playing the same music indefinitely, but if there is to be any change, any progress, any novelty, the creative mind is needed again; and so it is in industry. And, it may be added, the creative mind must be free to do its work.

To sum up, Marx was not a great thinker, but a great agitator—an agitator of the pen; and it is in that capacity he lives although his system is in ruins.[1] He had some of the gifts of a great thinker, but lacked the most important of all—originality. No well-informed student any longer claims for him the power of really original thought. Even the idea of 'Labour power' he seems to have got from Hobbes, whom he quotes on the subject.

[1] Since writing this I have learnt that Mr. Beer has expressed a similar opinion.

But besides lack of originality his temperament was incompatible with the character and function of the philosopher or pure thinker. There is abundant evidence in his own writings and in the testimony of men who knew him, including Mazzini and Bakunin,[1] that he was intellectually vain, overbearing, intolerant, jealous, suspicious, and eager for recognition. These are not the qualities of a great thinker. No great name in the whole history of thought can be cited as an example of them; they are entirely foreign to the character. But they are just the qualities that have been exhibited by many an agitator.

It is an arguable proposition that the agitator's function is the higher of the two. I shall not argue it, but will merely observe that agitation may be destructive or constructive, and that only the latter is of value to mankind; and the Marxian agitation was essentially destructive. He foretold and urged the overthrow of the existing order of society, but refused to give any guidance for the building up of the new. The essential change involved was the transference of the means of production from private to common ownership, which was the original object of the first Socialist society in England, as described in Chapter II. The difference of the Marxian conception lay in the assumed inevitability of the process and in the instrument for carrying it out, namely the class

[1] 'He called me a sentimental idealist and he was right; I called him a vain man, perfidious and artful, and I was right too' (Bakunin.) 'A man of acute but destructive spirit, of imperious temperament and jealous of the influence of others. He believes strongly neither in philosophical nor religious truths and, as I had reason to fear, hatred outweighs love in his heart' (Mazzini). Other contemporary judgments are still more severe.

war. The task laid down for Socialists was to arouse and cultivate class feeling, to inculcate, foster and promote the class war by every means.[1]

On this purely destructive aim of 'Down with Capitalism!' and on this alone, all were agreed. Endless differences about the manner of achieving it arose and persisted; nor could there be any finality, since warrant for every method, from the most gentle and gradual to the most sudden and violent, could be found in the ambiguous and inconsistent views of Marx and Engels, whose sacred writings were the ultimate authority. The microscopic examination, to which they have been subjected by rival exponents for recent controversial purposes between Bolsheviks and Social Democrats, shows that they sometimes took one view and sometimes another; they agreed neither with each other nor with themselves, but swayed backwards and forwards.

On the constructive side—on the form which the new economic order was to take after the abolition of Capitalism, still greater uncertainty prevailed because they said very little about it, and what they did say was very vague. The proletariat were to seize political power, whether by force or by

[1] Some ingenious person, knowing that the cult of the class war is obnoxious to many Socialists in this country, has recently promulgated a new reading of it, according to which it is not waged by 'Labour,' but by the 'ruling classes' against 'Labour.' This completely reverses the ideas of the originators and preachers of the class war. The declared aim of the Communist Manifesto is the 'forcible overthrow of existing social conditions,' and so late as 1890 Engels called the Socialist movement 'the attack on the ruling classes,' adding that the Socialism of 1887 was almost identical with that of the Communist Manifesto. Since the entire mass of enabling and remedial legislation, which, it is admitted, has greatly strengthened 'Labour,' has been passed in every country by the 'ruling classes,' their method of waging war is certainly peculiar.

constitutional means, establish a dictatorship, wrest ownership from the bourgeoisie, who would disappear, after which thc State, as an organ of authority, was to 'wither away'—Saint-Simon's old idea in another form. This forecast is sketched in very misty outline and tells us nothing of the future organisation of society and the manner in which economic life would be carried on. The excuse for silence on a matter so important and so necessary in order to convince reasoning minds of the desirability of the change was that, according to the dialectical method, the coming of the future state was inevitable, and therefore to describe it would be a useless and superfluous undertaking. Why the same argument does not apply to the destructive class war campaign is not apparent.

Nevertheless, both Marx and Engels did here and there discuss certain problems of the future and drop a few indications of what they expected. So far as these go, they exhibit a degree of Utopianism far exceeding that of any of their despised predecessors.

Take, for instance, workshop control and discipline; how would they be managed in a state of perfect equality? Marx thought that discipline, which is necessary under Capitalism, would be superfluous in a society where workmen work on their own account, as it is almost superfluous today on piecework.[1] Engels, who knew more about works' management and the co-ordination necessary for the conduct of industry, took a different view. He did not discard discipline, but got round the difficulty by abolishing the differentiation of

[1] *Das Kapital*, III, p. 57.

functions. Work, he says, will be a pleasure; managers and tub-shovers will change places every half-hour, and in this way the labourer will submit to discipline for a short time in order to direct the work himself immediately afterwards.[1] He had the delightful vision of every man as an equally capable Jack-of-all-trades, ready to play the architect and wheel the barrow alternately.

Further, there would be no market, no buying and selling, and consequently no money. Production and consumption would be exactly balanced and, in the language of economics, exchange value would disappear and only use value be left. The time required for the production of the various commodities would be fixed by 'society,' which would also distribute the labour power and means of production to the different branches of industry. How these proceedings would be carried on without the re-introduction of authority and discipline is not explained. The Bolsheviks, who have tried the experiment, have made some discoveries about it.

To continue, distribution and consumption would be carried on under the system by means of labour notes. Every man would receive a note entitling him to draw from the communal stores an amount corresponding to the labour time he had put in.[2] Here we have a combination of the Saint-Simonian principle, 'From each according to his capacity, to each according to his works,' with Owen's system of labour exchanges.

[1] *Anti-Dühring*, pp. 213, 320.

[2] Marx, *Misère de la Philosophie*, p. 54; *Das Kapital*, II, p. 331, III, p. 388; Engels, *Anti-Dühring*, pp. 335–6.

But neither recognised the principle of equality, which was to be established by the Marxian system. How was actual equality of consumption to be secured between individuals of unequal capacity under a system of equal pay for equal work. Marx recognised the difficulty:

> 'The right of the producers is in proportion to the work rendered; equality consists in their being subject to the same measure—namely, work. But one man is physically and mentally superior to another, and, consequently, does more work in the same time, or can work a longer time; and work, if it is to be the measure, must be estimated in proportion to its length or intensity. This equal right is unequal right for unequal work. It recognises no class distinction, because every worker is in the same position, but it tacitly recognises the unequal endowment and capability as natural privileges. It is, therefore, a right of inequality.'

This passage occurs in a posthumously published letter written in 1875, and criticising the Gotha programme. It shows that Marx anticipated the familiar criticism based on natural inequality, and that fact ought to be known to students of Socialism. But what was his solution of the problem? That these natural privileges of unequal capacity are due to Capitalist society (not to Nature), and must be put up with in the first stage of Communist society; but in a higher stage they will disappear, and absolute equality will prevail—not only social, but mental and physical equality. To which vision may be added another hardly less remarkable transformation. The distinction between town and country will be abolished.[1] What would happen to the seaports and river-side towns we are not told, but perhaps the distinction between land and water will also be abolished. Nothing seems impossible in this wonderful communist society, in which men will all be exactly equal in body and mind.

One cannot help reflecting that Marx was fortunate in not living in a society in which all his contemporaries would have been his intellectual equals.

[1] Engels, *Anti-Dühring*, p. 314.